From Students

"*The Reason to Sing* is an imperative addition to technique. This is one of our greatest masters giving you a master class on the practicalities of acting through song. Enjoy stepping into his classroom. It's a magical place to be."

Annaleigh Ashford

"Craig Carnelia taught me how to act. He has an uncanny ability to reach the heart of a song and the heart of his students. His students are not just singers. They are storytellers."

Sutton Foster

"Craig saw promise, intelligence, and capability in my acting before I could acknowledge or value those qualities in myself. Through his gentle encouragement and disarming honesty, I was offered a safe place to explore every facet of myself and examine those facets until I learned to love and respect them."

Barrett Wilbert Weed

"Simply put: I owe my career to Craig – every audition, performance, award nomination and accolade. He gave me the confidence-of-self to sing each note and lyric with purpose, truth and integrity. His class will forever be my Northstar."

Brandon Uranowitz

"Craig's teaching left an indelible mark on my acting and in my writing. I still hear his voice when I approach new material or a new role. Oh, and I booked a lot of Broadway shows because of his class."

Jennifer Sanchez

"Throughout my seven years of studying with Craig, I observed his uncanny ability to introduce the artist to themselves. He would consistently intuit exactly what each student required to use their entire being to tell truth through art. His role in my life has been immense both as an artist and a human."

Laura Dreyfuss

"Craig's teaching changed the course of my career. The work we did together re-shaped the relationship I have with song and gave me permission to 'not perform' and to trust that I am enough. Craig's work creates an environment of vulnerability and honesty which results in searingly poignant communication between artist and audience. Beginning with my work in Craig's class, I was able to build on that and have ended up in some of the smartest and most courageous rooms in New York."

Beth Malone

"I've had the great pleasure of taking Craig's class on and off for many years. His unique approach to musical theater acting, through personalization, relationship, and storytelling, has the ability to unlock even the most difficult of acting challenges. He was crucial to my finding confidence and useable tools as a young actor, and I still think of his class often, across all mediums of my work."

Aaron Tveit

"Craig Carnelia is perhaps the most influential teacher in my study of musical theatre. Coming from a strictly classical music background, I only understood acting on a performative level. Craig broke me of the habit of 'just singing' and freed me to *communicate* through song."

Elizabeth Stanley

"Encountering Craig's class was a pivotal moment in my journey as an actor. He has an uncanny ability to observe his students and draw out their truths by responding to what is most human in them. He is deeply present with his students, and that level of presence is something I continue to aspire to in my work and life."

Ato Blankson-Wood

"I could write a book. Craig's teaching is simultaneously tangible and visceral, yet also meditative and beyond the confines we set for ourselves. I cannot recommend him enough and hope this book inspires the creation of more studios and communities such as the one he created on West 72nd Street."

Erika Henningsen

From Universities

"This book is wonderful! Craig Carnelia offers a clear methodology, a step-by-step process to discover surprising authenticity and originality in the acting of songs. He has illuminated a supportive, insightful and inspiring acting process that creates the illusion that this master acting coach is standing by your side. It's this intimate collaboration between the author and the reader (the teacher and the student) that makes this book so uniquely valuable to the student. I intend to use no other textbook in my Music Theatre Techniques class at Northwestern University from now on."

David H. Bell, Director of Music Theatre, Northwestern University

"As a master teacher of Musical Theatre, Craig Carnelia cuts to the heart of songs and makes them immediate for young performers. He espouses an admirable balance of insightful interpretation, emotional acting and crisp musicality. His master classes are always highly anticipated events at CCM."

Aubrey Berg, Chair Emeritus, CCM Musical Theatre Program

"Craig Carnelia is something of an industry standard in the teaching world regarding this subject. Utilizing the very best of Meisner, Stanislavsky, Uta Hagen and several other master teachers, his distillation of these ideas is profound, simple and accessible. A master instructor in his own right, there is something here for every aspiring and established singing artist."

Robert Westenberg, Professor of Theatre and Coordinator, BFA Musical Theatre Program, Missouri State University

"Craig Carnelia is *the* Master Teacher of Acting a Song. Elon's Music Theatre students have been very fortunate to participate in and observe his many master classes on campus. Everyone leaves his classes inspired and carrying with them unique and valuable tools for their next performance. I trust you will be similarly inspired by *The Reason to Sing*."

Catherine McNeela Nt.D, Professor of Performing Arts and Coordinator of Music Theatre, Elon University

THE REASON TO SING

In *The Reason to Sing*, renowned composer-lyricist and teacher Craig Carnelia provides musical actors with a step-by-step guide to making their singing performances more truthful, vivid, and full of life.

Using a technique developed over decades of teaching the professional community of Broadway actors and students alike, *The Reason to Sing* utilizes detailed descriptions of sessions the author has had with his notable students and lays out a new and proven approach to help you build your skills, your confidence, and your career.

This book is intended for musical theater acting students as well as working professionals and teachers of the craft.

Craig Carnelia has taught acclaimed musical theater acting classes for the Broadway community for over 25 years, as well as frequent master classes at many top universities including CCM, Elon, Northwestern, University of Michigan, and Missouri State. As composer-lyricist, he has received two Tony Award nominations, two Drama Desk nominations, two Best Plays citations, the Johnny Mercer Award, and the prestigious Kleban Award. His shows include *Working, Is There Life After High School?, Poster Boy,* and (with composer Marvin Hamlisch) *Sweet Smell of Success* and *Imaginary Friends*. Best known songs include *Flight* and *What You'd Call a Dream*. He is currently at work on a new musical with book writer John Weidman.

THE REASON TO SING

A Guide to Acting While Singing

Craig Carnelia

Routledge
Taylor & Francis Group
NEW YORK AND LONDON

First published 2021
by Routledge
52 Vanderbilt Avenue, New York, NY 10017

and by Routledge
2 Park Square, Milton Park, Abingdon, Oxon, OX14 4RN

Routledge is an imprint of the Taylor & Francis Group, an informa business

© 2021 Craig Carnelia

The right of Craig Carnelia to be identified as author of this work has been asserted by him in accordance with sections 77 and 78 of the Copyright, Designs and Patents Act 1988.

All rights reserved. No part of this book may be reprinted or reproduced or utilised in any form or by any electronic, mechanical, or other means, now known or hereafter invented, including photocopying and recording, or in any information storage or retrieval system, without permission in writing from the publishers.

Trademark notice: Product or corporate names may be trademarks or registered trademarks, and are used only for identification and explanation without intent to infringe.

Library of Congress Cataloging-in-Publication Data
Names: Carnelia, Craig, author.
Title: The reason to sing / Craig Carnelia.
Description: [1.] | New York : Routledge, 2021. | Includes bibliographical references and index.
Subjects: LCSH: Musicals—Instruction and study. | Singing—Instruction and study.
Classification: LCC MT956 .C37 2021 (print) | LCC MT956 (ebook) | DDC 783/.043—dc23
LC record available at https://lccn.loc.gov/2020044558
LC ebook record available at https://lccn.loc.gov/2020044559

ISBN: 978-0-367-27241-8 (hbk)
ISBN: 978-0-367-27242-5 (pbk)
ISBN: 978-0-429-29572-0 (ebk)

Typeset in Joanna MT Std
by Apex CoVantage, LLC

This book is dedicated to my students

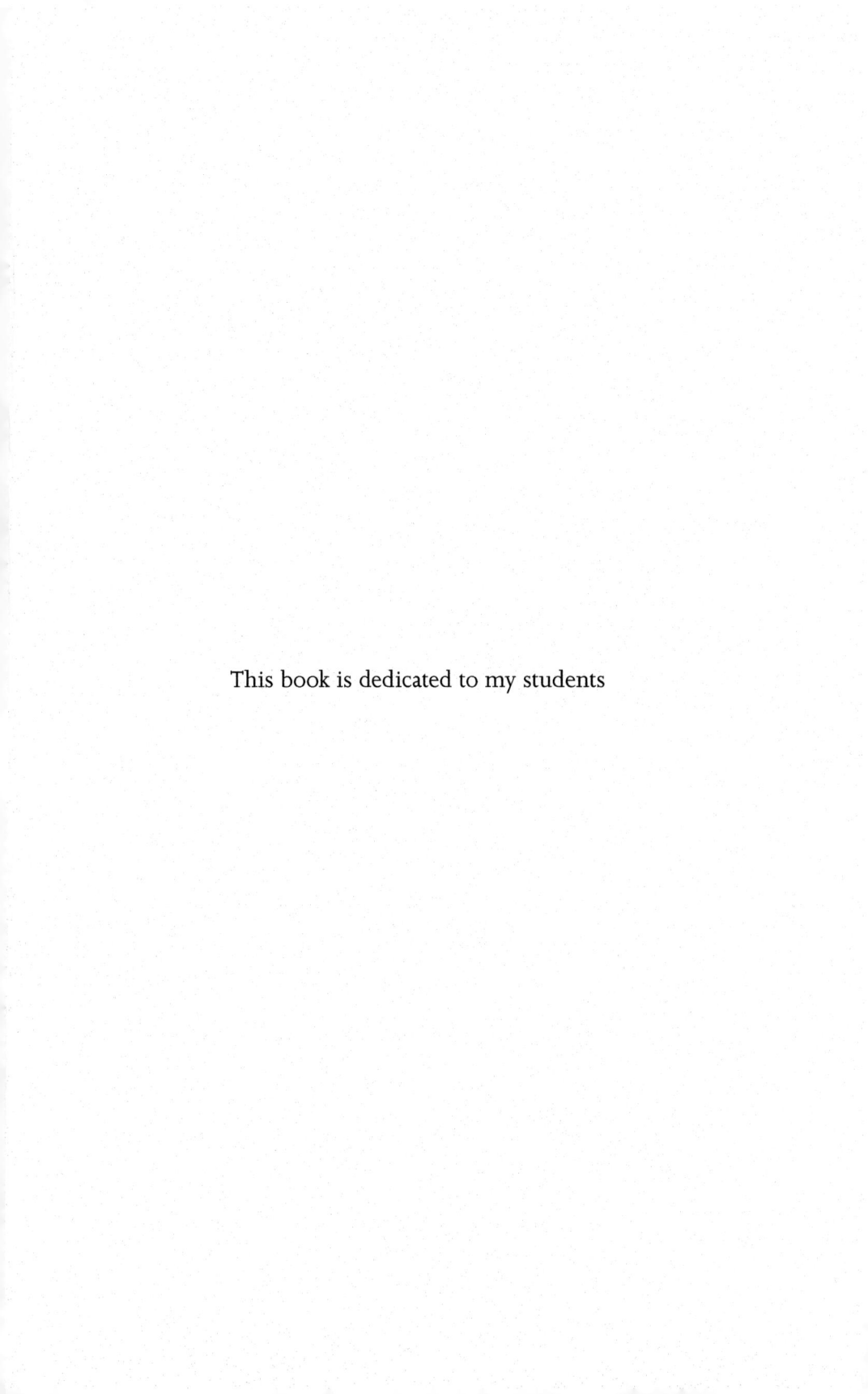

CONTENTS

	Acknowledgments	xiii
	Preface	xiv
1	**Approaching the Song**	1
2	**Preparation**	19
3	**Action**	34
4	**About Music**	53
5	**Types of Songs**	76
6	**Invisible Partners**	102
7	**Auditioning**	107
8	**A Sense of Play**	116
9	**In Production**	123

What does this do to her? How has her body responded to this touch? Not her head, her body. And how is her blood moving? So much of theater music is about this, the rate of the heart, the blood, and how they are different this minute than they were the minute before. This is what has happened and this is why she sings.

"Anyone Can Whistle"
From "Anyone Can Whistle" (1964)
Music & Lyrics by Stephen Sondheim

Unlike the "Wild Party" song, which is full of detailed imagery, and the "My Fair Lady" song, which is deliberately general, Sondheim's 1964 ballad is spare, deep, and poetic. This is a simple song about a complex person who has mastered many a difficult task while coming up short at the simpler aspects of life. It can be sung by anyone and approached in countless ways. We'll only look at this one out of context of the musical, since that is how it is almost always used. On the one hand, the song is so simple that it seems to tell you how it should be approached. On the other hand, it seems to be asking you to "fill in the blanks."

The first word you need to define is "whistle." What do you mean? You might mean "whistle," but chances are there is some aspect of life, some natural, human act that is or has been difficult for you, such as trusting, loving, letting yourself be happy, letting yourself be successful, or even relaxing at auditions.

The second blank to be filled in is the word "you." Looking at the second half of the lyric, we see: "Maybe you could show me how to let go." Who is the "you?" There is so much room for experimentation here. You could try any number of people. It's very possible that your first impulse is best. But I've also found with this song that there may be someone you haven't considered who would serve you even better. It might be a partner, friend, parent, sibling, mentor, or someone of less obvious importance. Be open to surprise in this type of exploration. Try different approaches, and in the process, you will give yourself multiple times through the song, and if you truly engage in each exercise, it's an excellent way to build muscle and flexibility as an actor.

As for action, it sounds like you're admitting, acknowledging, perhaps for the first time, that you have this limitation and are asking for help with it, though you may or may not know when you begin that you're going to ask for it.

All of these questions may seem daunting, but in reality they could all be boiled down to a single line from "Measure for Measure:" "Go to your bosom, knock there, and ask your heart what it doth know."

You already know these things. You already have these answers. You just probably haven't put them to work for you in the acting of your songs. Going through this process of questions and answers can give you a better reason to sing than simply having a general sense of what the song means to you. When you ask yourself questions, you get answers, answers full of detail. And *detail unlocks feeling*. This is how we write, and this is how we act. Given the unique qualities of "Anyone Can Whistle," if you simply define the words "whistle" and "you" and take a good, slow breath to clear away everything else, the song will probably do the rest of the work for you.

"Desperado"
(Country-Rock 1973)
Music & Lyrics by Glenn Frey and Don Henley

The two best recordings of this song are by The Eagles (with Don Henley's lead vocal) and Linda Ronstadt.

According to both dictionaries I use, a "desperado" is "a bold, reckless criminal." The songwriters are using this word in a figurative sense, about a person who is some sort of "emotional outlaw." Many of you have heard this song at some point, and some of you may know it well. Either way, please take a moment and read through the lyric, or listen to one of the two recordings listed above.

Look at how much you already know. You already know who the desperado is. And you also know why he, she or they need to hear this.

And that's the way you most likely should approach the song. But look again. These things you "know" aren't actually in the song. They're in you. What may have seemed obvious at first glance is not obvious at all. It is your own personal view of what is going on in the song.

It's useful to become conscious of such things as you explore your material. It's not unlike the experience we've all had hearing a song we've known for years and one day it speaks to us as it never has before because of a situation we're currently in. "Oh! *That's* what this song is about."

I've even had this experience with songs I've written. "Oh, *that's* where this came from!" Stephen Sondheim has told me he's had the same experience with songs of his. As writers, we sometimes know things we don't consciously know. I believe this is true of actors as well.

Now, let's change gears and use "Desperado" for an entirely different purpose. In the preface of this book, I spoke about the actor wishing to make a particular type of impression ("I don't want it to be too angry / They're looking for someone ethereal / This is my sexy song") and how aiming at such targets can lead to pretending. Well, sometimes, choosing how to approach your material can give you an organic way of bringing forward the very qualities you know the character to have or those emotions you may have been clumsily asked to "present" in some result-oriented direction.

So, looking at the Frey/Henley song, the desperado is either you or someone else, right? As an exercise, I'd like you to now make a different choice than the one you originally gravitated to.

If singing to yourself now, is it the present day, or was there a time when you most needed to learn this lesson? And what did not having learned it yet cost you?

If singing it to someone else, who would that be? Is the desperado a friend of yours? Why do they need to hear this?

Is the desperado a lover, or possibly an ex? Why couldn't they or can't they "let you love them?" Was it a question of timing? Did you think it was your fault, that you somehow weren't good enough? Were they still in love with someone else? And by the way, did the ex end up attending your wedding? Or did you attend theirs? Such a detail could unleash a storm of feelings within you. And such a storm could be very useful.

Or how about this? Was your father or mother absent or incapable of loving? Could one of them qualify as a desperado? If so, what did this cost you?

And look at how different the song would be when sung to yourself, to a friend, to an ex, to a parent.

Considering the variety of approaches "Desperado" might offer you, one could organically slant this smart song toward roles in "Violet," "Big River," "The Robber Bridegroom," "The Spitfire Grill," "Bright Star" or anything else it might be appropriate for.

* * *

I'd like to take you to my classroom now. It's on West 72nd Street, between Amsterdam and Columbus, at a branch of Ripley/Grier Studios. We're in Studio 4R, which is on the top floor in the back of this smallish building. The stairs are unusually taxing for people, even 20-year-old dancers. I've always suspected that the vertical spacing between the steps is a bit greater than we're accustomed to. However, I chose the top floor so there would never be noise above us.

The door is red, the walls are lavender, the floor has a Marley surface for dancing. One wall is covered with mirrors; another is one big window. Across the gardens and alleys between 72nd and 73rd, we see the backs of brownstones on 73rd Street. Above them, sky – lots of it. A pigeon once committed suicide against our window during someone's song. Through that window, we see it start to snow in winter and hear and see the rain year-round. On bright days, we turn off the overheads and work in natural light. On these days, if the sun moves behind a cloud, the light in the room changes. This often happens mid-song. It is magical. I taught four classes a week in this room from 1992 through 2017.

March, 2007

Aaron Tveit is working on an audition for a new musical being produced at Second Stage called "Feeling Electric." He has been given a song to learn for the audition called "I'm Alive." In it, he plays a young man singing to his mother while she is in a therapy session. The young man exists only in his mother's mind, having died as an infant. The therapist is one of many she has seen over the years in an effort to deal with her grief and the bi-polar disorder that was triggered by her infant son's death.

Aaron gets the part. The show by Brian Yorkey and Tom Kitt gets retitled "Next To Normal." It then goes through a second production in D.C. and opens on Broadway, all under the expert guidance of Michael Greif.

But back in the classroom, how to approach the song? We decide to use two of Aaron's classmates as partners, one as the mother and another as the therapist. Later in the session, we will remove the partners. But for now, they sit facing each other in a hushed, improvised dialogue, while Aaron uses the song to try to get his mother's attention and to convince her that the therapist and everyone else are wrong, that he is still with her, right behind her, real, necessary, and alive. All of this information is in the song.

What isn't in the song is this: does the character have free will or, being in the mother's imagination, is he somehow controlled by the limits of her thought process? We decide on free will, because if the character doesn't have this, his actions are not his own, and the way in which those actions are controlled by the mother would almost surely lead to a stylization of some sort. As an actor auditioning for the role, such a choice could easily be read as the actor himself being less alive.

We also work on not letting the infectious tone of the chorus music ("I'm alive, I'm alive . . .") woo the actor away from his purpose in the scene. Yes, the tone changes but the action remains.

September, 2010

Leah Horowitz is preparing for her final callback for the role of young Heidi in Eric Schaeffer's upcoming production of "Follies" (music and lyrics by Stephen Sondheim, book by James Goldman).

The song "One More Kiss" is an homage to the operetta style that had been one of the staples of musical theater in the early decades of the 20th century. The lyric has a surface meaning that speaks of love, but the song has a deep resonance that embraces the entire event that is "Follies," and the ache these characters feel for the lost days of their youth.

As of this date (September, 2010), Leah has been in six Broadway shows and had countless other first-rate jobs. She is always working. But actors tend to think, as each job ends, "Was that the last one I'll ever get?" Leah chooses to use this as her motivation, and the depth it brings to her performance brilliantly matches the author's intentions.

She had to leave class early today, to get to the callback. She sang right before leaving, and the gorgeous high D-flat she had just sung was still hanging in the air as the door closed.

We all just looked at each other and said: "That's her job."

And it was!

March, 2016

Brandon Uranowitz has been in class for five years. He's always had a great affinity for the songs of William Finn. Over the years, we've worked on "Anytime," "What More Can I Say?" and (on multiple occasions), "Mark's All-Male Thanksgiving."

Brandon had a major professional breakthrough in 2015, when he played Adam Hochberg in Christopher Wheeldon's production of "An American in Paris."

Today, he brings in "A Day in Falsettoland" and "A Marriage Proposal," to prepare for his final callbacks for the role of Mendel in the upcoming Broadway revival of "Falsettos."

Mendel is a clinical psychologist, and in the first song, he is in a session with a patient he finds soul-less and exhausting. I give Brandon a scene partner, who makes up an ongoing monologue as he sings. His action is to block out the dull hum of his patient's complaints about life while venting his own.

For "A Marriage Proposal," Brandon makes reference to a time early in his own long-time relationship when things began to get serious. Mendel is smart and articulate. His brain is always there for him. In this scene, it is not.

Brandon thinks he may use the reader at the audition as a scene partner. So, we work on the song both ways, with and without a partner, to get him ready for either choice.

January, 2013

Liana Hunt recently finished a 2-year run as Sophie in "Mamma Mia!" at the Winter Garden Theatre. She is auditioning for "Newsies," to replace Kara Lindsay in the plum role of Katherine.

In the play, Katherine writes for a newspaper as a fourth-string theater critic and reporter of other inconsequential stories. In hopes of elevating her status at the paper, she is researching and writing a serious piece about the boys who scratch out a living selling newspapers on the streets of New York in 1899.

The boys (or newsies) have gone on strike to win a slightly higher profit from each paper they sell. They are led by Jack Kelly, a cocky, handsome boy of 19 or 20. The owner of the paper is wealthy and powerful and also happens to be Katherine's father. No one has asked her to write this story, and in fact, the subject matter runs contrary to her father's political views and business interests.

She has much to prove in this situation: that she is a good writer, that she is worthy of more important assignments at the paper, that a woman can be a serious reporter, and that the boys' cause is just and should be supported. Put simply, she wants to change her life and save the world.

In the song "Watch What Happens" (music by Alan Menken, lyric by Jack Feldman), Katherine is attempting to accomplish all of the above while plagued by moments of both insecurity and grandiosity, and distracted by stray thoughts of the cute, overconfident boy who leads the newsies. Menken and Feldman have craftily peppered these multiple distractions throughout the song to interfere with the character's ability to write her story.

The tendency for actors in this song is to live in the anxiety, the frenzy of ambitions, insecurities and distractions the writers have given her. So, Liana and I work on the simplest of possible approaches. I ask her what the character is trying to do, not what she's *doing*, what she's *trying* to do. "She's trying to write a good story." "Exactly. Try to write a good story. The song will do its best to interfere with that aim, as you try to stay on track."

Watch someone who is very, very drunk. You'll see that they are trying to act sober, to not slur their words, to walk in a straight line. This character, who is very, very anxious, is trying to walk in a straight line toward *her* objective.

And that's what Liana did for the next year at the Nederlander Theatre.

September, 2016

Alex Finke has just been cast to play Johanna in the immersive production of Sondheim's "Sweeney Todd," set to open off-Broadway at the Barrow Street Theatre. We had worked on "Green Finch and Linnet Bird" before, for her auditions for the show, but she wants to look at it again with rehearsals coming up.

In the play, Johanna has grown up as the ward of Judge Turpin, who years earlier had exiled her father (Sweeney Todd) to an Australian prison camp for a crime he did not commit. Having gotten Sweeney out of the way, the judge then preyed on Johanna's mother sexually, until he tired of her and threw her out into the street, where in the years that have passed she has become a crazed beggar woman. Johanna is coming of age, and the judge has now set his sights on her. He keeps her in captivity in his house, where her only companions are her caged birds. In the song "Green Finch and Linnet Bird," she is singing to the birds, asking them how they are able to live in such seeming contentment in captivity.

We talk about the character and her stunted life experience and go looking for a reference in the actor's own life where she might have felt thwarted, held back, or even captive. "Adolescence." "Yes. Adolescence, times 100." Because everything in "Sweeney Todd" is times 100. Another reference, a relationship or period of time in which the actor might have felt dominated or suffocated? "Yes." That, times 100.

This is a character who finds her life intolerable and is looking anywhere she can for an answer. So how does Alex approach the song? She prepares by putting herself in the character's situation and then takes action by literally doing what the song says she is doing: asking the birds how they are able to survive and even flourish in a cage, so that she too can possibly survive.

* * *

A classic love song by Jerome Kern and Dorothy Fields from the musical film "Swing Time" . . .

"The Way You Look Tonight"
(1936)

There are two people in the scene: the person who is singing and the one who is being sung *about*. The person being sung about can either hear the singer or not, your choice. In both of the examples that follow, the second party does not hear what the singer is saying/thinking.

Ato Blankson-Wood sings this song in class about his then boyfriend coming down a grand staircase at The Met. Ato is so enraptured by the sight, he wants to "press pause."

Kevin T. Collins sings the same song about a recent evening when his wife, Meghann, had a stomach flu. She was sitting up in bed, having just vomited, and he couldn't help but marvel (even in *this* situation) at her beauty.

* * *

One of Sara Bareilles' terrific songs . . .

"Gravity"
(2007)

Sara Bareilles' pop songs are as actable as good theater songs. It was not surprising, then, that she made her musical theater debut so artfully and successfully with "Waitress." This song, about the downward, gravitational pull of a relationship, is one of her early pop songs.

Student "A" sings about an ex, while student "B" sings about her career. For student "C," the song is about something in herself that causes her to plummet emotionally. And the alphabet of possibilities continues.

* * *

A song of mine from "Diamonds," an off-Broadway revue about baseball, directed by Hal Prince . . .

"What You'd Call A Dream"
(1984)

I had become a baseball fan in my late 20s but had never played any organized sport when I was a boy. As I wrote this song (in my mid-30s), I pictured two different ballfields: the sand and pebble field at the public high school I attended on Long Island, and Yankee Stadium. The two fields were somehow fluid in my thoughts as I worked.

In the song, the singer recounts the details of hitting a game-winning home run. The song can be sung about "something that happened" (a dream come true), or "something that didn't happen." The choice is yours to make but is never voiced in the lyric. Either way, the best action for the song is simply "telling the story."

Robert Creighton played shortstop and catcher when he was a boy, but he was not much of a hitter because he was afraid of the ball hitting him. He sings to the class.

Devon Goffman played third base and batted second. He sings to us about a particular hit he got that won a game when he was 12 years old. He remembers exactly how it felt when the bat connected with the ball.

Jaime Rosenstein was the catcher on her softball team in middle school and draws upon the imagery of that team and that field in telling the story. But what she's really singing about is the night her father came to see her play Nessarose in the national tour of "Wicked."

Noah Zachary played third base in Little League. His father had been the coach of the team but died when Noah was 4, before he began playing. In such a context, it becomes all the more important to simply "tell the story." By keeping the action as "practical" as possible, the unspoken part of Noah's story can inform the performance without dominating it.

* * *

Now, choose a song for yourself (anything at all), and let's see how you want to approach it. For any of you who just thought of a song and instantly second-guessed yourself, don't. Go with your first idea. Even if trusting yourself feels foreign, it's only because you've had so much practice doing the other. You've picked a song. Good. Take a moment and think or read through it, if you would.

Do you envision yourself as being alone in the song or are you with someone else?

If you see yourself as alone in it, what does that mean to you? Would you be singing to yourself, or to the universe, or perhaps to the "idea" of another person?

We talk to ourselves all the time. Remember what it felt like the last time you did this? It's almost as if there were two of you, or two halves of you. This is what singing to yourself can be, not a contemplative rumination, pointed inward, but something as active as talking to another person.

And what if you're singing to the universe? How do you define the universe? From what I've witnessed in class, it's possible that we each think of it differently. Is it planets and stars and space? Is it people? Is it nature or energy or some idea of God? Whatever it is to you, just putting it into words makes "singing to the universe" more specific and meaningful than just saying: "I'm singing to the universe."

If you're singing to the "idea" of another person, why have you chosen this person for the song? Or was the choice inevitable? And why now? Or are you placing yourself in an earlier time?

The above questions are not intended to be a list of set questions or rules. Rules can be comforting, but comfort is not the aim here. The aim is to look at the acting of songs in a new way, to approach them with greater depth and specificity, to ask questions – the ones I have posed or ones that may suit you and your song even better.

As your teacher, I might know where to poke and prod you, but you know even better. So, poke away. You're looking to touch a nerve, to ignite yourself with feelings of joy, rage, fear, love, frustration, whatever might be called for.

You think someone's following you on a dark street, your chemistry changes. You're about to tell someone you love them for the first time, or finally let go of a crushing disappointment, your chemistry changes. This is what we're looking to do in our preparations.

2

PREPARATION

Preparation is commonly misunderstood and misspent. All too often, actors will take a moment to prepare and merely end up reacquainting themselves with the subject of the song, or perhaps the cast of characters it involves. These things are important, but they are more the work of the last chapter, "Approaching the Song," and they will tend to leave the actor unchanged. The very purpose of preparation is to cause change, to transport you from where you are emotionally to where you need to be, so that the action you then take in the song has a visceral reason to be taken.

Failed preparations may take the form of what I call "tipping your hat" to the subject, as if merely referring to it would prepare you. Or they may be quite the opposite and have a determined concentration about them, where you are actually working quite hard to prepare. I've frequently heard that someone is "working to get to a feeling."

This is the actor's stance we often see parodied; the "serious" actor taking a strained moment of intense concentration before beginning. It's easy to parody because it can look foolish and always fails.

But a good preparation needn't feel like work at all, and it's not "the feelings" you need to recall but something that will cause those feelings to occur within you. In life, when we are taken from the reality we're in to some other emotional state, our brain is engaged for the briefest of moments, but then the rest of the body gets involved, and not by working at it. Our blood, our chemistry, all those fluids that make up the greater part of our body weight, actually do the work, and they do it naturally.

Let's say you're attracted to someone. The eye tells the brain and the brain tells the rest of you, all in a heartbeat. And if this occurrence is at all meaningful to you, you take a sort of snapshot of it. As an actor, if you need to be filled with that feeling again, you don't try to recall the feeling; you simply look at the snapshot. It's in your head.

What we're attempting to do in a preparation is to "allow" this to happen, never to force it, to draw upon imagery or detail that will bring about this chain reaction. A breath is always useful in this process, a deep breath, to clear away the clutter. Then, imagery and detail can work their magic on you. You may sift through a variety of images to find the one that best triggers you and you may also find you sometimes need to choose different imagery as time passes.

If you're playing a role, it's very possible that the flow of the play will lead you naturally to a song. Still, you may find that some songs are triggered best for you by an overlap of text and your own experience. This is part of how the writing was done. These characters, if they're well written, are part of the author. I don't mean the plot is autobiographical. But your character, its fiber, is partially made out of who the author is. And when you're playing the role, it's made out of who you are too.

* * *

Here's an example of what I just described, how a personal preparation may be melded with the text when playing a role.

"The Wizard and I"
From "Wicked" (2003)
Music & Lyrics by Stephen Schwartz

One of my students was working on this song while preparing to play the role of Elphaba. Elphaba is one of those rare parts where the character's arc in the show is so complete and compelling that the text itself (by Schwartz and book writer Winnie Holzman) feeds and supports the actor at every turn. Yet while working on "The Wizard and I," my student found that a personal trigger worked best for her in this song.

We are in the Land of Oz. In Elphaba's first scene, she arrives as an incoming student at Shiz University and is met with the same derision she has encountered all her life, due to the fact that her skin is a vivid green. As the scene unfolds, she inadvertently displays one of her extraordinary powers (psychokinesis), which makes a huge impression on Headmistress Madame Morrible. Morrible (who is also a sorceress) tells Elphaba that she will write at once to the Wizard, to tell him all about her, and she predicts great things for the girl.

Madame Morrible exits upstage as Elphaba watches her go. After a moment, alone onstage, she turns and asks herself and the wind: "Did that really just happen?"

My student was reminded of a moment years earlier when she was sitting at her office job of ten years and got the call that she had landed her first Broadway show. She was truly in a state of disbelief and found herself saying things on the phone like: "So you really want me to be in your show?" She played Elphaba some three or four hundred times and made use of this as her preparation for "The Wizard and I" throughout that experience. After her preparation, the actor's flexibility and the richness of Schwartz' writing easily allowed her to slip back into the character's shoes and simply be Elphaba for the rest of the song. But the preparation and the jolt it provided were from *her* life, not from Elphaba's.

* * *

One of the greater challenges in choosing and using preparations can be the actor's reluctance to go to bad places when necessary. The case

I just cited with "The Wizard and I" called for traveling to a pleasurable moment that would cause great, good feeling in the actor. The employing of such preparations takes practice and craft, but there is little emotional danger in doing so.

When the danger increases, it is quite common for actors to employ their preparations less successfully, out of fear of what they might feel or fear of having such feelings in front of other people. An actor may also deliberately or subconsciously avoid this danger by choosing a reference for their preparation that won't really hurt and, hence, won't really work.

Let's look at a common situation: a romantic loss and one of Irving Berlin's timeless standards.

"What'll I Do?"
Music & Lyrics by Irving Berlin (1923)

We'll use just the refrain for this one. In the song, a couple has parted. The singer is pondering how to live without the other person. But they're not just *pondering*; they seem to be *asking* the other person (the one who is no longer there) what to do. "What'll I do?" "How do I stop imagining who you're kissing?"

Working on this song with a new student, she began by trying to access what she had felt four or five years earlier when she broke up with a longtime boyfriend. She was currently in her best and happiest relationship ever and found it difficult to exhume her ex, for a variety of reasons. "It was so long ago." "By the time it ended, I don't know if I even still loved him." "I'm so happy with John; it's hard to feel that now." And so on. Her heated resistance to using the ex could have signaled that this was the perfect choice for the song, but given the newness of the student and what I knew to be the potential of the song, my instincts told me otherwise. So, I suggested we invent a breakup with her current boyfriend, John.

"But things are so good between us, I can't imagine breaking up." What she really meant was: "Things are so good between us, I don't *want* to imagine breaking up." It's precisely because things are so good that this might be the right scenario for the song.

Ten minutes into our work on "What'll I Do?" it became clear that the choice of scenario was not really the issue. The student simply needed to summon the courage to put herself in *any* uncomfortable scene, whichever one she might choose.

You must be willing to go to bad places, to know everything you actually know and not shield yourself from unpleasant feelings. There's an expression I don't quite believe in that says: "That which doesn't kill you makes you stronger." In the arts, it is probably true. It's how we know how to write, to paint, to act. And as artists, we need to use anything and everything that might ignite us, to let ourselves access this treasure trove of emotion we hold the key to.

We chose to create a fictitious breakup with her current love; because of the two acting challenges, this was the simpler choice – simpler because she already carried half the preparation around inside her, in the love, heat and expectation that went along with this relationship.

The other half of the preparation would be "to believe in the breakup." For any actor in this situation, this is the part that takes courage because you don't *want* to believe in it. But if you have the willingness to go looking, you will find the detail that takes you there.

Most couples know what it is that would break them up, if anything did. It's bad, it's true, and it's yours. It's not that difficult to imagine this issue building up and causing a split. Or you could use a time when you *almost* broke up. We all have them. They usually end with tears and reconciliation. But before that, we live the experience as truly as if the break had actually occurred. Or perhaps you're the type of person who believes that every argument means the end of the relationship. Many of us are. If so, here's a chance to make use of this neurotic fear. Because in the fear, we've seen the end. We've already lived all of this. Why not put our morbid imaginations to work for us?

Ask yourself questions about the breakup. Make it real for yourself. If it did occur, who would leave, who would stay? Where does the one who leaves go? Be specific: whose couch? Is there contact between the two of you after the break? How soon? Who *are* they kissing now? Do you know? Does the person look like you, or are they everything you think you're not? Do you still sleep in the bed you shared? Is there a restaurant you'll be avoiding? Details. Until something fills you with this feeling.

For me personally, settings or pieces of settings are deeply evocative. And scents. For others, it might be the time of year, or the time of day, or sounds, those in the background, or perhaps an article of clothing. The color of the sheets is more likely to take you to the scene than the color of the lover's eyes. I don't know why. Be open to anything. There are countless details available to you in any situation, and in the case of "What'll I Do?," one of them will put a dagger in your heart. And that's what happened that day in class.

* * *

Finding the right detail for a preparation may take some work, but once found, the rest is often easy.

Here are two examples, out of hundreds, of a single detail leading an actor to a deep preparation.

"Is It Really Me?"
From "110 in the Shade" (1963)
Music by Harvey Schmidt
Lyrics by Tom Jones

A longtime student was working on this song, from one of the best scores of the 1960s, to possibly add to her audition book. In the song, the person singing feels beautiful for the first time because of what she sees in her partner's eyes.

I asked the student what her experience had been with what the song is describing. "I didn't think I'd find this in my life, and I have." She sang, and the performance was sincere and attractive but no more than that.

So, I asked her if she'd ever actually had the *unique* experience that in her lover's eyes she could see that she was beautiful. "Yes." "Where exactly?" "Sitting on the leather couch." Instantly, she was filled with something deep, complex and subtle, something that then illuminated both the song and the singer. In the bargain, her voice had a more distinctive sound. It was not just a good voice; it was *her* voice, something that could not have been achieved through technical means alone.

Obviously, the leather couch in and of itself was not responsible for my student's good acting and singing, but locating the setting of this emotional experience caused her to be filled with what she had felt in that setting, which then resulted in a performance as gorgeous as the song.

* * *

In "The King and I," Tuptim (a young Burmese woman) has been presented to the King of Siam as a gift from the Prince of Burma, thus becoming one of his possessions.

She and Lun Tha (an emissary from the court of Burma) are in love. This love is forbidden and must not become known. Lun Tha sings to Tuptim.

"We Kiss in a Shadow"
From "The King and I" (1951)
Music by Richard Rodgers
Lyrics by Oscar Hammerstein

A student brought this song to class and wanted to relate it to his experience as a gay man. As potent as the student's idea might have been, his first performance was similar in its lack of depth to the first performance of "Is It Really Me?" and probably for the same reason – a lack of specificity in the preparation. Not surprisingly, then, the solution was also the same.

I invited him to find a single moment when he was aware of having to keep his love and his true self hidden. "Three years ago, in Boston, walking my college boyfriend to the bus terminal. I went to hold his hand and he pulled away, saying he didn't feel safe doing that in this neighborhood."

The resulting performance was tinged with anger, defiance and hope, to go along with the love and longing we're accustomed to seeing in this great song.

Detail unlocks feeling and feeling gives you the reason to sing.

* * *

In each of the last two examples, the actor was prompted by the teacher to find a more specific and personal situation to help them relate to the song. But looking more closely at how the teacher knew what to ask each of them, we see that the writing itself offered those clues.

"Have you ever had the unique experience spoken of in the song, that in your lover's eyes you could see that you were beautiful?" Tom Jones (the song's lyricist) told me where to go looking, in his second verse.

The point is, the student didn't really need the teacher, she just needed what was on the page and what was in herself. And it was the raw information and deep texture of Hammerstein's lyric that showed me how to coax the second student to a richer performance of "We Kiss in a Shadow."

You see, the detail that unlocked the feeling in each of these cases was originally put there by the writers, before either of these students were even born. But then it was their turn to study the text, to analyze the lyric, so they could find their own detail to once again open the lock.

Could reading the entire plays "110 in the Shade" and "The King and I" also have been useful? Of course. As an actor, it's useful to read as many plays as possible, but in these two cases, all the pertinent information necessary to act these songs brilliantly is right there in the music and lyrics.

Conversely, if you were to sing the song "Old Maid" from "110 in the Shade" or "My Lord and Master" from "The King and I," reading the full play would be a necessity. These songs are rooted in their stories and characters to such an extent that the context they were written for is as much a part of the writing as the music and lyrics.

* * *

Now, let's look at two contemporary songs – one from the pop world, one from the theater, each of them richly actable. Both are stories, so both would profit from being sung to other people, real or imaginary, individual or group. The first needs only a simple preparation; the second, a more involved one.

"My Stupid Mouth"
Music & Lyrics by John Mayer (2001)

This song is usually sung by a man, but it can work well for any gender.

The person telling this story has a long history of saying the wrong thing, or saying too much, and has just done so last night at dinner with a date. The lyric is full of beautifully observed detail of the tragic dinner and the singer's self-recriminations about not thinking before speaking, about having no filter. It starts right out by telling us the problem: "My stupid mouth has got me in trouble. I said too much again. . . ." So how might you prepare for this?

In your catalogue of memories, some of the hardest to shake are those moments when you've made a hideous social blunder. Just as we replay those delicious moments in life when we found precisely the right words, we torture ourselves with replays of our faux pas, embarrassments and humiliations.

As an exercise, think back to one of your blunders. Relive it. When we do this, we cringe, visibly or not. This visceral reaction is all the preparation you need to fuel this funny pop-song.

* * *

The second contemporary story-song is similarly full of humor and self-mockery, but it speaks of a darker experience.

"And They're Off"
From "A New Brain" (1998)
Music & Lyrics by William Finn

In "A New Brain," Gordon is in the hospital for an emergency craniotomy (brain surgery). A "family history" is required for his medical chart. Gordon sings of family outings to the horse races, his father's gambling addiction, domestic violence, financial ruin, and abandonment.

This song would not only profit from having an audience (group or individual), it actually needs one, because the character so clearly wishes to entertain with this tale of his dysfunctional childhood. Like many of Finn's characters, Gordon has undoubtedly had lots of therapy, and it hasn't worked.

So, this is what he does. He makes an ironic vaudeville of the pain and chaos of his childhood. When I say "vaudeville," I'm not suggesting a performance style that speaks of old-time performing. Not at all. In fact, the telling of this story should be quite naturalistic and true-to-life. But the character is lit-up from within about his subject, and he's using irony to separate himself from it.

Singing the song outside the play, how might you prepare for it? You're way ahead if you come from a dysfunctional family, and having made a study of this, I would estimate that seven out of ten actors have this advantage.

If this is true of you, you probably don't need any help remembering the highlights. But on the chance your memory needs a jog, look to those two great family pressure cookers, the dinner table and the car. Think back over your family experience in those two settings and you will likely find the fireworks. Speaking of fireworks, holidays are a great place to go looking for trouble, especially the ones late in the year.

Now, try to tell the story of those family fireworks aloud to someone. And here's the challenge: don't feel sorry for yourself. It's your own personal train wreck, and you can make a game out of how you talk about the wreckage. Tell your tale as if you were dining out on this travesty with a friend. Try it.

Now, having experimented with telling your own twisted tale this way, try singing the song from this perspective. That's what the writing seems to be asking of you, and the writing itself will help you do it.

But what if you're one of those actors who had two good parents and a happy childhood? Nearly every example given thus far in this book has called for some version of using one's own life experience. What do you do if you've never experienced anything like what you're being asked to inhabit?

This is certainly not the only answer to this very big question, but in the case of "And They're Off," you probably had a close friend or perhaps a cousin who came from such a habitat. Even if you never witnessed the dysfunction in all its glory, you knew the house and you knew the parents, or at least you saw them passing through. I had a friend in junior high whose parents were both alcoholics, a fact I didn't know until we were in our forties. But there was a spare bedroom upstairs that became so cluttered with junk that one day his mother, who was always in a bathrobe, nailed it shut. And it stayed that way. The dominant smell of the house was something like "wet dog," though they had no pet. Once, while we were playing with my friend's chemistry set in a dank basement lit by a single light bulb, we ducked under a makeshift clothesline strung with underwear, and my friend held a lit match to his sister's bra until it started to burn. The house was crazy!

So, if I didn't have my own one-of-a-kind nuthouse to draw upon, the vibe I got in *his* house and my imagination would allow me to step into his shoes for the song. But not just imagination: empathy, because through him, I could feel the sickness of the house. During the bizarre scene in the basement, it occurred to me that my friend wasn't worried the burn mark would raise questions or, if it did, that anyone would ask him about it. Empathy is a great tool for the actor, as is fantasy, and to some extent, paranoia and even delusion. They're all ways of living experiences we haven't actually had.

And it's possible to empathize with *any* character, not just those with whom we have a natural affinity. Imagine this: a kid (say 10 or 11 years old) races feverishly down the middle of the street on a bike, seemingly in a panic. Thirty feet behind, three other kids race by, clearly in pursuit. Ten feet behind them, a fifth passes, part of the group but somehow laying back.

Which one of them do you relate to? Do you identify with their situation, their actions, their place in the sequence of five bicycles? If so, you probably also relate to what they're feeling, to the point where you almost feel it. Watch the scene again, and let yourself take the place of the kid you relate to. Close your eyes if it helps.

The song that character would sing would come from that feeling. The writer would make the song out of it. And the actor would sing from it, using just such a preparation. In this instance, empathy would probably take you about two-thirds of the way there. The rest of the distance could be covered by imagination.

I saw the scene I just described in my early twenties. The reason it stuck with me is that as I watched it unfold, I thought: "I would have been the first kid or the last." The first, being chased by the pack, filled with terror of what would happen if and when they caught up with him, and the last who didn't want to be part of what the pack was doing but didn't want to forfeit membership in the group altogether.

But what about the pack? What if we needed to inhabit one of those characters as a writer or actor? It's very possible that some of you did identify with them, in which case, the greater challenge for you would be in relating to numbers one and five. But for the purpose of this discussion, I'm going to assume that most of you identified with the first or last.

Given that assumption, the challenge for us would be in empathizing with the three in the middle. To begin with, let's say that this "pack" is actually three individuals choosing to do the same thing. So as an actor, you are not Pirate #2 or Toxic Cheerleader #3, acting cruel and bloodthirsty for no good reason.

What prize is there to be won, what discomfort alleviated, what pleasure experienced by being part of this group? Do you have a grievance, real or imagined, with the kid you're chasing or are they just a pawn in a game you're playing that then allows you to be one of the bigger chess pieces? It feels good to be one of those pieces, doesn't it? Have you ever deliberately overlooked what the prey might be feeling so you could enjoy the pleasures of being more powerful?

And maybe it was hard to gain entry to this pack. Do you really want to give it up by not participating in the chase or, worse yet, by switching sides to help the underdog?

In baseball, when your teammate hits a home run, do you empathize with the opposing pitcher? Perhaps, if you're a pitcher you do. But what about those 40,000 cheering fans? Are they 40,000 bullies or 40,000 individuals who've traveled as many different paths to this moment and are feeling elated, even if the opposing pitcher is on his way back to the minor leagues at the age of thirty-six and soon to be out of the game of baseball entirely?

What I'm saying is: there are ways to understand and access any character, any situation. And villains never know they're villains. In their story, they're the hero.

** * *

Even if the song you've been handed to sing lacks the authenticity and subtlety we've been talking about, you can bring a deeper dimension to your performance by acting the song they *didn't* write. Wait! You can act a song that's un-actable? Yes, you can. There are many situations where you may be given such a song (for instance, an audition, workshop, concert or even a production), a song that defies your ability to use the tools we're discussing here.

This happens often with workshops because the songs haven't been tested yet, or because the shows themselves may lack the quality to go any further than the workshop stage. But it can also happen because the writers aren't aiming for the kind of stage-worthiness we're talking about, perhaps because the songs were written to be on a recording and not a stage, or perhaps the writers have an ethic or an ambition that causes them to eschew the very qualities that would make their songs actable. Whatever the cause, you will most surely find yourself in this situation as an actor, and here are two ways to handle it.

If the song is in a musical, look at the song-spot. What is happening? What is the character trying to do? Even if the writer hasn't made use of these elements, the actor may be able to. If the situation your character is in is full of life but the song is not, act the situation. Or rather, find your action in the situation.

Another way to come at this problem is to study the lyric, looking for clues. Somewhere in there, there is probably a good line or a good idea, possibly one that even suggests action. When there's a good line in a poor lyric, or an active line in an inert song, it can usually be found near the beginning or the end. *That* line suggests the song the writer might have written. You can act that song, the one they didn't write. It's all in how you approach it, in your preparation and your action.

* * *

Sometimes, a physical state can help lead you to the right preparation. I did say earlier that in preparing to sing "it's not the feelings you need to recall but something that will cause those feelings to occur within you." But sometimes, the physical state itself can cause those feelings to flow.

If you need to be breathless with anxiety, you can run up three flights of stairs, or do however many push-ups would tax you in this way, then sing. Yes, you will be winded, but you won't be *pretending* to be winded. You can then cut back on the amount of physical exercise you engage in so that you are not unduly compromised by it, but this technique can teach you what it is to actually *be* in this state for your song.

If you need to be in a state of surrender, lay on your back on the floor. Close your eyes, open your arms, and let yourself melt into the floor. Sing from there. Then stand and sing the song again. The sense of surrender will more than likely still *be* there.

If you need to be dizzy with emotion, twirl in circles until you are physically dizzy, then sing. After the dizziness has passed, sing again.

A good, emotional preparation could lead you to a similar state, but the physical state itself can sometimes be helpful in your preparations.

* * *

In their process, writers will often ask themselves and their collaborators questions not unlike the questions I've been asking you, the actor, in this chapter.

In 1964, John Kander and Fred Ebb were writing the score for "Flora, the Red Menace," with George Abbott and Robert Russell writing the book. The legendary producer Harold (Hal) Prince had assembled this team with Abbott, a veteran of countless Broadway successes, as director, and Kander and Ebb, a pair of newcomers working on their first musical together.

The plot of the show concerns Flora, a young visual artist living in New York City during the Great Depression. Early in the show, she applies for a job as a fashion illustrator at a department store, which would pay her thirty dollars a week and change her life. The job application is cleverly musicalized in an introductory verse with Flora singing both the questions and answers, the final question being: "Reason for applying for this position?" This leads her to the body of the song: "All I Need is One Good Break."

A few scenes later, she gets the job. The songwriters needed to musicalize the moment, but they got stuck. They couldn't figure out what Flora would do or say in this momentous situation. I, of course, wasn't there; I was on Long Island watching my friend set fire to his sister's underwear, but I imagine they were stuck because they were thinking of the situation as momentous, just as earlier in this chapter my students were thinking too broadly by singing about finding love or being gay. Remember the leather couch and the walk to the Boston bus terminal?

So, Mr. Abbott asked the young songwriters: "How did you feel when you got this show?" And Fred said: "Of course."

The team of Kander and Ebb went on to write fifteen musicals, including "Cabaret" and "Chicago," but the song "A Quiet Thing" from their first show remains one of their very finest.

Seven blocks south of where "Flora" played, more than half a century later, "Dear Evan Hansen" opened on Broadway. A few days after her opening in the show, Laura Dreyfuss was in class singing "A Quiet Thing" to her longtime classmates. The truth of what Kander and Ebb had given Flora to sing in 1964 was alive in Laura that Tuesday afternoon in 2017.

I'll finish this chapter by reprising a line from the chapter's first paragraph. "The purpose of preparation is to cause change, to transport you from where you are to where you need to be, so that the action you then take in the song has a visceral reason to be taken."

3

ACTION

What you're feeling and what you're doing are two different things. Action is what you're doing, not physically but emotionally.

Sometimes the action of the song will be easy to identify by analyzing the text. This doesn't mean you have to play that action. But if the writing is good, it's probably wise to accept this invitation from the author.

Just as often, the action will be hidden or completely open to interpretation.

The curious thing is that, in any of the above situations, the emotion of the song can very often steer you away from the action.

"Far From the Home I Love"
From "Fiddler on the Roof" (1964)
Music by Jerry Bock
Lyrics by Sheldon Harnick

In the play, Tevye and one of his daughters, Hodel, are at the train station awaiting a train that will take her to be with her fiancé, who has been arrested on political charges and exiled to Siberia. Siberia is a frigid, barren place, far away from everyone and everything Hodel has ever known. Tevye doesn't understand how she could make such a choice. He has implored her not to go, and still, she is leaving.

The lyricist has offered a perfect action in his first line. Hodel sings to her father: "How can I hope to make you understand?" Everything she then says and does is an attempt on her part to accomplish this task. Yet having worked on this song with dozens of young women who were auditioning for or preparing to play the role, I've seen very few gravitate naturally to this action.

Here's why, I believe. Hodel is feeling many things, among them, love (for her father, her family, and her fiancé) and a great sadness to be leaving home. And though Sheldon Harnick's superb lyric is set to equally superb music by Jerry Bock, the music speaks most persuasively of the sadness in the scene, so that the overriding aura of the song is that of a lament.

But "lamenting" is not her action, and sadness and love aren't actions at all; they're feelings. She may *have* those feelings, but she also has a fervent wish to be understood by her father before the train gets there. It is this wish that drives the song, not her sorrow. If she can make him understand in the time they have left, both father and daughter could possibly have some kind of closure before parting and a greater chance for happiness in the future they're each facing. This is what she's fighting for.

So just as Harnick searched for what Hodel might say to make Tevye understand, *she* is searching for what to say to accomplish this same task. Whatever she might be feeling, she is engaged in a task, a practical action, amid the chaos of her emotions.

* * *

Practical action gives purpose to a song and infuses your performance with the vibrance of true behavior. You begin taking action because of what you're feeling, and as you continue, those feelings shift, overlap and evolve just as they do in real life. This variety of color in the performance occurs naturally, not through planning, but through preparing effectively and then taking action. By characterizing the action as "practical," I in no way mean to downplay the importance or passion of the situation. It's just that those aspects of the situation are *why* the action is taken; they are not the action itself. With practical action, a song being sung to God becomes an attempted communication instead of an act of reverence, and a love song can be someone trying to express the inexpressible, instead of an attractive, heartfelt interlude.

A song to God . . .

"How Glory Goes"
From "Floyd Collins" (1996)
Music & Lyrics by Adam Guettel

A young man explores a heretofore undiscovered cave. Through a series of cave-ins and mishaps, he is trapped under rock and rubble. After more than two weeks of failed rescue attempts, in his final moments of life, he sings to God.

The lyric is a series of questions about what happens after death, what it will be like, where it is we go.

As dramatic and beautiful as the original context is, the song itself is so surprisingly universal that it can be successfully taken out of that context. Outside the play, which is how the song is most often used, the conditions that are so vital within the show (the cave, the cave-ins, even the fact of the character being near death) are not necessarily vital to your ability to sing and act the song well.

Here are two ways to approach this piece out of context. When someone close to you dies, where do they go? You have ideas about this, even beliefs, but you don't know. Still, you sometimes find yourself talking to that person, don't you? When you do that, do you have an expectation of being heard? Whether or not you do, you can sing "How Glory Goes" this way.

Or you can sing it to God. But what if you don't believe in God? Consider this: when you're figuratively brought to your knees by circumstance, do you ever talk to the ceiling or just the plain air around you? Clenched in a heap on the kitchen floor, at a total loss for how to go on, do you sometimes utter a word or two, like "Please" or "Help me?" To whom or what are you saying these things?

So, in this song, you can sing to someone who has died, or to your idea of God, or to the absence of God you may believe in. Even *that* is a belief.

Not knowing if you can be heard doesn't diminish the action; it intensifies it. You're trying to communicate, not knowing if the entity you're singing to can hear you, or even exists.

An element that increases the difficulty of the task is often called an "obstacle," and it can be extremely useful in defining your action and playing it. Many acting teachers believe, in fact, that there should *always* be an obstacle. What I believe is that there is most often one, but not always. Sometimes, the obstacle is written into the scene/song, as in "Far From the Home I Love" and "How Glory Goes." Sometimes you may *add* an obstacle by how you interpret the song, such as in the action I'm proposing for this next piece.

A love song . . .

"Younger Than Springtime"
From "South Pacific" (1949)
Music by Richard Rodgers
Lyrics by Oscar Hammerstein

Adam Guettel's grandfather, Richard Rodgers, wrote this beautiful ballad with the great Oscar Hammerstein.

So, here's the situation. Handsome, stoic Lieutenant Cable loves Liat, a beautiful, young island girl. They're alone, and they've just been intimate.

Unlike the "Fiddler" song, this song's action is not prescribed by the first line of the lyric, or any line of the lyric. So, what is he doing, and what are *you* doing when you sing this song?

To begin with, the language is extremely poetic. Hammerstein was famous for this style of writing, as in "You are Love," "All the Things You Are" and others. But the presence of poetry is not a signal from the author to perform the song with a generalized romanticism, as so often happens.

I believe that theater writers intend for you, the actor, to become the author. I don't mean we want you to change what's written. We don't. What I mean is, in most cases, your character has never said these things before. So just as Harnick and Hodel are engaged in the same task by trying to figure out what to say to make her father understand, Hammerstein and Cable are each in the position of trying to express the inexpressible to Liat. This challenge helps your action, just as not knowing if you can be heard helps your action in "How Glory Goes."

Becoming the author of the song, inventing it as you go, is all the more important when the language is poetic, to bring it down to earth (where we live) and get it out of the clouds. I'm not suggesting that the song and its sentiment are small or mundane. They are, in fact, extraordinary; they just aren't *lofty*. If you also consider that what you feel for the other person in "Younger Than Springtime" is so good and so uncommon as to be inexpressible, then what you're doing is *attempting* to express it. What you're not doing is rhapsodizing, the very thing this type of poetry can tend to promote.

It's January of 2009. I'm in class with Andrew Samonsky, who has just taken over the role of Lt. Cable in Lincoln Center's long-running revival of "South Pacific." Working on "Younger Than Springtime" with Andrew, we begin by putting the insights from above to work. Then we go further into exploring the character and the context. We talk about war and what it must be like to live with death on a daily basis, and how Cable guards his feelings, to the point where he may not even feel them anymore. And we continue to look beyond the poetic style of the writing to find what the character is truly trying to say. He's telling Liat that he has been transformed by her, transformed and perhaps even saved.

An oasis is not just a nice spot with a small pond and a couple of palm trees; it's a life-saving pool of water and a patch of shade in the middle of a desert. The oasis is given its very definition by the desert. So, when you sing about having found such a thing, you bring the desert you've just crossed with you.

This is what Liat is to Cable, and in or out of "South Pacific," I believe this is what Hammerstein is expressing in "Younger Than Springtime."

* * *

The first three songs referenced in this chapter were sung to other people, or in the case of "How Glory Goes," to another entity. In this song, the character is singing to herself, the universe, and her sleeping lover.

"Changing My Major"
From "Fun Home" (2014)
Music by Jeanine Tesori
Lyrics by Lisa Kron

The play's main character, Alison, is a cartoonist who comes from a deeply troubled family, where the trouble is concealed behind a carefully maintained facade. She is played by three different actors to show the character at three different ages: 9, 19 and 43.

In this scene, Medium Alison is a freshman in college and has just had her first real sexual experience. She has known or suspected for much of her life that she was gay, and last night she allowed herself to have what she had long been craving.

It is morning, and her lover is still asleep, which allows Alison the space and privacy to freely process the extraordinary events of the night before, and process them she does.

One student who was working on an audition for the role had conveniently experienced a coming-out scene at 20 that was strikingly similar to this. Another made reference to a particular boy in her past, saying: "He was my first everything" (thank you, Cara O'Brien). For another, this was how she felt with someone new, after finally liberating herself from a repressive four-year relationship that had begun in high school. In each case, the student had known the exhilaration and release of having emerged in this way, as if she were now declaring: "This is who I am. I'm going to be *me* now."

So, wherever these young women found this in their experience, tapping into it for this scene proved to be a potent preparation. Similar to the prep needed, the action of the song couldn't be clearer; Alison is sifting through what has happened, how she feels about it, and how she now plans to live her life. And please note, as you study this song, there is no obstacle. You could invent one, but why would you?

I referred earlier to "letting the song do some of the work for you." Assuming you've prepared and you know what you're "doing" in a song, this is almost always a good idea. In this song, it certainly is, because the writing unfolds in such an unexpected manner, as the character careens from tangent to tangent, and discovery to discovery. Your job, then, is to *let* it unfold, line by line, section by section, feeling your way through this thrilling new terrain in your life.

"Changing My Major" is a long song, one that develops in a sprawling fashion, but Kron and Tesori didn't know when they began writing it how long it would be. So, on the theory that you, the actor, are now the author, you too have no way of knowing what the shape, size, and build of the song will be when you begin.

As I write these lines, I am engaged in a very strong action. I'm trying to make a point, one I care a great deal about, one I've made many times in class but have never written down. I'm writing this passage with the energy of that action, and I have no idea how many words it will take to fulfill my objective. This is true when we write, and it's true when we act. You don't know how long your song is going to be or how it will unfold any more than you know in Act I what will happen in Act II. And this great song is a perfect illustration of how "not knowing" can serve both the writer and the actor.

* * *

"I Can't Make You Love Me"
Pop-Country song (1991)
Music & Lyrics by Mike Reid and Allen Shamblin

The lyric of this classic song offers you a powerful action, but once again, the music and the situation are so emotional that the action can get lost in the smoke.

Looking at the text, it's unusual for a pop song to have such a strong backstory. Everything this couple has been through with each other is present in the song. Equally impressive is that the backstory is not even spoken of, it's implied.

Here's the unspoken history. These two people have been involved for an unspecified amount of time; it could be months, it could be years. During that time, the singer has loved more and loved better than her partner. They have fought almost as often as they've made love, and they've made love frequently and passionately. They have broken up numerous times, each time getting back together for more of the same. The singer probably believes that her lover somehow holds a magical key to her heart and her passions that no one else will ever possess, so that if the relationship were to end, this magic would be gone from her life forever.

And yet, tonight is different. Whatever has just happened: another fight, or the same fight, or perhaps her sister has finally convinced her to end it, or maybe the partner has just admitted to cheating yet again. Whatever it is, tonight they both know it's really over.

So, here's what she does: she asks her lover to stay the night so that she can experience the narcotic of this love one more time. And look what she offers to try to get this: a promise not to cry or even object to being the only one in the bed who's in love, and a vow that she has truly surrendered to reality and won't make any further fuss in the morning.

That's an astounding action, yet the situation itself is so intensely emotional that the specificity of that action can be obscured by it, and often is. It's the actor's job to not let that happen.

*　*　*

I met Lin-Manuel Miranda in June of 2009, when we taught together for a week at the Johnny Mercer Songwriters Project at Northwestern University. I had seen "In The Heights" and been instantly struck by the freshness of Lin's writing and was also impressed and moved by the understatement and heart of his performance.

Other than teaching songwriting that week, we played a lot of foosball, made each other laugh, and shared the stage in a couple of concerts. The first of them was in a tiny off-Broadway style theater in downtown Chicago. At this concert, Lin sang an early version of the opening sequence from a hip-hop musical he was writing called "The Hamilton Mixtape."

The writing was, of course, the writing: a brilliant opening for what would become a landmark musical. But the performance had as sharp an action to it as the best acting we see in musical theater. He was "telling a story," and he wanted it to be heard. Simply that.

Throughout this book, we are examining the relationship between the writer's work and the actor's. Well, Lin-Manuel does both of those things. But I can tell you that what I saw that night in Chicago was this: the writer was acting the song.

Acting and writing, writing and acting; mirror images of one another.

* * *

Musical theater is a mash-up of opera, vaudeville, jazz and every style of popular music from big band to rap. So, it's no wonder that musical theater acting is often treated as the bastard child of acting and entertaining.

When we first find ourselves interested in acting in musicals, through being in a show in high school, or singing along with cast albums, or from being drawn in while watching a live production of some kind, we usually begin by "performing."

This comes partly from the misconception I cited earlier, that acting is about pretending to be someone else. But we have also learned to "perform" from watching music videos, award shows, animated films, parodies on SNL, opera broadcasts, MGM musicals, cartoons, Elvis Presley movies and anything and everything else we may have fallen in love with or been exposed to.

Added to that, different teachers embrace different styles of acting, as do different directors, and no two musicals are alike either. You may find yourself auditioning for, or cast in, a show that actually relies on a mix of performing and acting, or that needs some sort of cartooning in order to come to life. So, given all the mixed signals we get about what acting is, it's not surprising that most of us begin by pretending.

I'll often hear from a student who has just broken through in their work in class: "I feel like I'm not doing anything." What they're not doing is all the "stuff" they had been doing to indicate what a person might look and sound like if they were truly engaged in their song.

What sense does it make that we exhibit expansive, varied, uniquely physicalized behavior every minute of the day, until we're onstage, at which point we stop being genuine, so we can control the look and sound of the product? And yet, this is what many actors do.

Despite any lessons you've had to the contrary, the audience isn't there to see you try to have an effect on them; they are there to see something have an effect on *you*.

* * *

I think of artists as list-makers who jump off cliffs. It's what we writers do, and I believe it's what actors need to do as well. We make lists so we can fly.

As I write this, it is the spring of 2019, and my wife, Lisa Brescia, has been on Broadway in "Dear Evan Hansen" since last summer, when she replaced Rachel Bay Jones as Evan's mother, Heidi.

Before beginning rehearsals last summer, she studied the play and the score and worked on the singing demands of the role with her vocal coach. Once rehearsals began, she worked during the day with a world-class team, including any and all of the following: the director, associate directors, stage managers, musical director, music supervisor, associate choreographer and cast. At night, she would watch the show or stay backstage, writing a personal biography for the character, full of invented background detail that isn't in the play. After the show, she would often walk through the scenes in our living room as I read the other roles.

So much of the process I just described is one kind of list-making or another, memorizing, drilling, practicing, getting ready, so when she's actually onstage she can jump off a cliff. The list-making makes this possible. And the "jumping off?" It's what we've been discussing in this chapter: taking action, not knowing what you're going to feel or what's going to happen next.

* * *

"Could be . . . who knows?"

"Something's Coming"
From "West Side Story" (1957)
Music by Leonard Bernstein
Lyrics by Stephen Sondheim

Here's a song where the music tells you as much about the action as the lyric. Tony, the character who sings this song, lives in a culture where the prospect of having a successful adult life is dim. He has grown up poor, in a street gang, high-school educated at best, never straying far from the neighborhood. And yet, he has gotten a job (menial, but a job), he has quit the gang, and he has a sense that his life is about to open up in some extraordinary new way.

Most young actors live in a suspended state where they work, hope, and wait for their next job. They do this despite the odds, believing in the transformative power of being cast and knowing that it can happen at any moment. My point is that most actors carry the prep for this song around with them.

And the action is so clearly expressed in both the music and the lyric that it's all but impossible to miss. You're reaching for this thing, you don't even know what it is, but it's right up ahead, you're almost there. The music itself is a study in syncopation, a rhythmic device where the syncopated note falls before the beat, in anticipation of the beat, as if the person singing can't wait to get there.

Even with all that clarity, I've seen two roadblocks come up as actors work on this song. One, actors often think of the song as "iconic," even sometimes using the word to describe it. But the word is for theater historians, not for actors. For the actor, the song is new. It has never been sung before, not until you "make it up" to express what you're feeling.

The other roadblock is common and can be frustrating. I've worked with any number of young men who have played Tony and were directed in one way or another to act "young and eager" in the song. Tony is young, and besides that, there is no good way to *act* young. As for eagerness, the music itself is eager (see definition of syncopation). When the musical intro begins, if you're not already where you need to be, the itchiness of the music will take you there. It's meant to be "how you feel," and it will make you feel that way if you let it.

Both of these roadblocks are worth our attention because they're not exclusive to "Something's Coming." They are recurring issues that will come up again and again in your professional life.

Roadblock #1 – The history of the song, the role, or the original actor who played it need not intimidate you. Sutton Foster worked on "Gimme

Gimme" in my classroom right after it was written, before she ever performed it in "Thoroughly Modern Millie." In the years since then, on the same spot in the same room, I've seen talented young women approach the song as if they were about to climb a mountain. But assuming you've done the work, that you've learned the song, and dealt successfully with its vocal demands, your job is the same as Sutton's was: to sing the song vibrantly while actively engaging in the scene.

The challenges of "Gimme Gimme" aren't that it's well-known or that the actor who played the role won a Tony Award for it. The challenges are the same two things Sutton worked on in class in 2001: how to genuinely be making a decision in the introductory verse and how to live the long musical build of the song as an organic escalation of feelings. She, of course, did brilliantly with those tasks, but so can you. For everyone from Sutton Foster to the next high school senior who tackles the role, the tasks are the same.

I've heard any number of men refer to Sondheim's "Finishing the Hat" as a "bear." There are no bears, not "Soliloquy" from "Carousel" or "Defying Gravity" from "Wicked." I was lucky enough to be in the audience at Playwrights Horizons the night "Finishing the Hat" was added to "Sunday in the Park with George." Mandy Patinkin held a music sheet in hand as he sang it. Point is, the song was new. After that first exciting performance, his job would be the same one you now have, to make the song new each time.

I got to perform this song recently in a concert of writers singing the works of composers who had influenced them. I was surprised when nearing the end that it felt shorter than I'd imagined it would. Had I, too, thought of it as a bear? It sure seems that way. But in performance, I was not singing a big, famous song; I was engaged in an action, singing to the audience, telling them about this quandary. And I was trying to figure something out, which is what George is doing.

George has a blind-spot. He can't understand why Dot left him. He seems to believe that if she just understood why he didn't meet her emotional needs she wouldn't leave. But she *does* understand. It's not a lack of understanding on her part that causes her to go, it's the neglect itself. That's the blind-spot, the thing he doesn't know, and it drives the song. George doesn't get it, and unlike Millie in "Gimme Gimme," he *never* gets it. Every character from Magnolia in "Show Boat" to Hamilton in "Hamilton" only knows what they know. Everything else, they *don't* know.

Roadblock #2 – If you're fortunate enough to make a life for yourself in musical theater, you will often find you're in a situation where the style of the director, or the process of the musical director, or even the demands of the staging or production, seem to conflict with the way of working I'm proposing throughout this book. But you don't have to let these or any other factors impair your ability to act truthfully.

Let's look back at "Something's Coming" and what the actor might do when asked to project youth and eagerness. We talked about how the song already embodies these qualities and how as an actor you already live in the preparation, and that the action of reaching for this "something" is right there on the page, waiting to be accessed by you. But you've just been asked to aim at a target, to present qualities, and the *wish to please* could get in your way and keep you from employing the basic tools of preparation and action that, ironically, could bring about the very effect the director is looking for.

In any situation, you can let yourself be as smart as you are. You can even learn to translate a result-oriented direction like the one above into an actable one. A very smart student of mine was recently asked in an audition to "act angrier" at a particular point in a song. She was singing to an unseen man and was able to instantly reword the direction by telling herself to "really let him have it."

In every musical you ever do, there are moments where the demands of the staging must be folded into the acting of a song. My students have often brought these challenges to class.

It's March, 2015. Betsy Morgan is Kelli O'Hara's standby in "The King and I" at Lincoln Center. Knowing she is about to go on for a weekend full of performances, Betsy has brought "Hello, Young Lovers" into class. The stage of the Vivian Beaumont is a deep thrust with audience on three sides, so the song has wisely been staged with a number of moves in it to favor different parts of the audience at different times.

Betsy and I had worked on the song previously for acting, but today she wants to incorporate the staging to find ways to motivate each of the moves, a couple of which cover quite a bit of ground. "Why do I move to this new place?" "Why do I move there, then?" We explore different ways to answer these questions, running the song multiple times, with Betsy's classmates as the "King and I" cast, and with the staging approximated within the smaller confines of the classroom. Without this exploration, the actor would still be obligated to make the moves. But, if unmotivated, the physical actions could cloud, or even obliterate, what the character is actually "doing" in the scene.

If you're wondering why this issue wasn't dealt with at understudy rehearsals, there are countless details to be handled at these rehearsals, and the high priority items will always get the attention.

Now, let's say you're in a session with the musical director and they are concentrating on the sound they want or how to make that sound. This is not at all unusual, and besides, you do this very thing with your vocal coach all the time. So why is it any different here? For one thing, the relationship is different. The musical director is partially responsible for you getting and possibly keeping the job. This reality can lead to insecurity or, again, an overzealous wish to please, and people-pleasing is deadly. It is a false behavior, and in this situation, it kills your ability to really engage with the musical director, to learn, and to get better at what you're doing. It's as counter-productive in this setting as being defensive.

You don't have to be perfect at the moment, and the wish to be perfect will only get in your way. You can back up in your process and treat the vocal demands of the role as part of your groundwork, even if those demands come your way after you've been in rehearsal for a while, or even later, in performance. Slow down, go back, work on the singing when you need to. Then allow yourself to move forward once again in your acting. In most cases, the acting will help the singing, but there are occasions when you may have to favor the singing for a time.

Sometimes we're thrown a curve. Sometimes there's a cast change that disorients us, or we're handed a rewrite, or given a note that contradicts a note we got last week.

There's an organic solution to every acting problem, and it's your job to find it. It's there in what we do all day long: we evidence real behavior and real emotion while taking action.

* * *

How to act "denial . . ."

I have found only one effective way to act denial, and that is to be full of the thing you are denying before you begin. If you aren't, you will find yourself caught up in two false actions: pretending to feel the thing you're trying to deny, and then, pretending to deny the thing you don't really feel.

To illustrate, let's look at a song from "The Last Five Years."

"See I'm Smiling"
From "The Last Five Years" (2002)
Music & Lyrics by Jason Robert Brown

This whole score is a feast for the actor, a song cycle made up of intricately textured, theatrical songs. Because the songs are so full of plot and character detail, it's best to approach each song in the context of the show.

Jamie (a novelist) and Cathy (an actor) meet, fall in love, and get married. He is charming, driven, narcissistic, and addicted to attention and romance. She is attractive, articulate, lacking in self-esteem, and always looking to Jamie for her happiness. As the story progresses, Jamie is soaring in his professional life; Cathy is stagnating in hers. In this scene, they are in their fifth and final year together. Cathy has finally gotten Jamie to visit her at her summer stock job in Ohio. Their marriage has all but disintegrated, and they both know it. This is what she's trying to deny, this reality, and the uncertainty, terror, and rage it causes her to feel.

The first half of the song gives her ample opportunity to deny reality, even to the point of seemingly trying to get him to agree with the unreality she is putting forward ("See, we're laughing." "We're doing fine."). But his actions in the scene, all unheard by the audience, make it harder and harder for her to do this.

Looking at the text, we see that Jamie's visit was originally planned to be for the whole weekend. In the course of the song, it becomes clear that he is not going to stay that long, at which point she still assumes he's going to spend the night and see her show. Then she finds out he's not even going to do that; he's apparently just there for the afternoon, or perhaps just for this encounter.

So, she loses it, and I don't simply mean this in the colloquial way we often use this phrase. She actually loses something, her ability to deny what's true.

The song will *cause* you to lose this ability when the moment arises, but that can only happen if you've been honestly engaged in denial before that, and *that* can only happen if you're full of the thing you're trying to deny to begin with. It can be buried, this thing you don't want to know, these feelings you don't want to have, but it needs to *be* there.

I would imagine that Cathy may have even come into this scene having promised herself she won't lose it, but the scene forces her to fail. After her outburst, after ". . . en route to the sky, and I . . . ," she does the *other* thing she had least wanted to do. She shows him the very behavior that has caused him to stop loving her in the first place: she holds him responsible for her misery, blaming him for it and expecting him to fix it.

All of this wonderful theatrical spillage, the outburst and the behavior that follows, is made possible by her denial. The abrasion between what is true and what the character is trying to *make* true is powerful, and there's no way to fake it.

* * *

A math problem . . .

142 X 1,703 = _____?

Without using a calculator or paper and pen, can you solve the problem? Give it a try.

If you just engaged in the above exercise, you experienced two important states, ones that every actor needs to inhabit often in their work: "not knowing something" and "trying to figure something out."

Numerous times in these first three chapters, I have referred to what we know and what we don't know, all the way back to the first page of the Preface, where neither the writer nor the actor knew yet how to give voice to what they were feeling. I gave all of us the above math problem to remind us what it actually feels like to not know something. Because, as actors, we study and analyze the song, the play, the role, and become experts on things our characters have to then not know. So, how do we handle this?

A few pages ago, I wrote about George's blind-spot and that his not understanding how Dot could leave him makes "Finishing the Hat" possible.

"Finishing the Hat"
From "Sunday in the Park with George" (1984)
Music & Lyrics by Stephen Sondheim

Looking at my own experience singing this song, this is how I handled the task of "not knowing." I prepared by imagining I had just been left by someone very important to me. This stung. I personally might have responded to this feeling in any number of ways, but knowing how the verse begins, I allowed myself to respond defensively. "Yes, she looks for me. Good. Let her look for me . . ." Throughout the rest of the introductory verse, I allowed the twists and turns of logic and emotion in the lyric to lead me where they would.

Then, as the body of the song began, I took deliberate action, trying to explain my inability to give the other person what she needed while at the same time trying to figure out why she left.

Having prepared so that I might feel what George felt, I allowed myself to respond to the feeling as George would. Then, I took aggressive action and let the writing do the rest of the work. This left me no choice but to be George.

So, there are things the actor knows that the character doesn't, just as there are things the writer knows and the audience knows that the character doesn't.

The character doesn't know how to "whistle," or how to deal with the downward pull of their problem's "gravity." They think things like: "What'll I do?" and say things like: "How can I hope to make you understand?" To be the character is to "not know."

* * *

A dinner problem . . .

You're in a restaurant you've never been to. You're looking at the menu, trying to decide what to order. There's a time in this process when you don't know what to have, and then there's a time when you do know. In-between these two realities, there must have been a moment when you decided. What did that feel like? How did you do that? How do you play Millie?

"Gimme Gimme"
From "Thoroughly Modern Millie" (2002)
Music by Jeanine Tesori
Lyrics by Dick Scanlan

In "Thoroughly Modern Millie," a young woman comes to New York in 1922 from Kansas, hoping to find a rich man to marry (for instance, her new boss, Trevor Graydon III). Instead, she falls in love with the supposedly "un-rich" Jimmy.

In the introductory verse of "Gimme Gimme," Millie asks herself whether she should marry for money or love. The verse concludes with the question: "What kind of life am I dreaming of?"

After a brief pause, the body of the song begins: "I say Gimme, Gimme." Then, another "Gimme, Gimme." Then another, without the character having yet declared (or perhaps decided) what she wants. In the fourth line, she declares her choice: "That thing called love."

So, somewhere between the last line of the verse ("What kind of life am I dreaming of") and the fourth line of the refrain ("That thing called love"), she decides. How do you do that? When exactly do you decide? How do we ever figure out what to order for dinner? And why are we always genuine at the moment of deciding in a restaurant but sometimes less than genuine in that moment onstage?

In life, we are not trying to have an effect on an audience; we are trying to decide what to order. Onstage, we sometimes don't trust that they will *see* it, so we *show* them, thereby destroying the moment.

Kudos to dear Sutton, and to any other Millie out there who trusts that if she actually *does* it, we will *see* it.

* * *

Sometimes, it's easy . . .

"Moon River" (1961)
Music by Henry Mancini
Lyric by Johnny Mercer

This is my all-time favorite song. I introduced my now grown daughter, Daisy, to it when she was three years old. After I played and sang it, she said: "It's happy and sad at the same time." Indeed, it is.

The writers have been poetic; you don't need to be. You can be literal. Pick a river, preferably one you've spent a good deal of time with. Whether you meant to or not, there's a good chance you brought your dreams, ambitions, and troubles to that river. Even if you didn't, if you merely envision the river and sing the song, that's what will happen.

* * *

- What you feel and what you do are two different things.
- Practical action unleashes an array of color.
- Let the song do some of the work for you.
- Don't know how long your song is.
- Let it unfold.

These themes will come back in different ways throughout this book, as will the principles of exploration, preparation, and action. But it occurs to me that we haven't really talked about music yet. And we should.

4

ABOUT MUSIC

I believe that actors should learn the music and sing the words. When someone is "acting the music," what they are really doing is making a sound picture. The singing voice should be used to *express* feeling, not *replicate* it. This is best achieved by singing the words.

Hand in hand with this, I believe that every singing actor should study voice throughout their career. "Singing the words" does not mean singing less well or with a less developed vocal technique.

However, singing and speaking are more alike than we commonly think. To illustrate, please read that last sentence again, this time aloud. Even without hearing you read it, I can tell you that the sounds you just made had pitch and rhythm and that those pitches and rhythms could be notated as music. That music would be less melodic than most songs, but it would still be music.

Now, read these lines aloud, if you would.

*Granddad was a sailor
And he blew in off the water
My father was a farmer
And I his only daughter
I took up with a no-good millworkin' man from
Massachusetts
Who died from too much whiskey
And leaves me these three faces to feed*

This is the first verse of the song "Millwork" by James Taylor from the musical "Working." I chose the piece because it is written in an extremely conversational style, one that actually invites you to sing the words.

Please read or otherwise familiarize yourself with the music below.

"Millwork"
From "Working" (1978)
Music & Lyrics by James Taylor

ABOUT MUSIC   55

(lyrics under music: "took up with a no-good mill-workin' man from Massachusetts, who died from too much whiskey and leaves me these three faces to feed.")

As you can see, the music has more melody than your spoken version. By this, I mean that the rises and falls from note to note are somewhat greater than when you spoke the lyric, and the musical lines are balanced with each other in such a way as to create a discernable melody, but the overall effect is that of someone talking to us.

Fittingly, this is also the song's action: telling a story to the audience. Singing the words allows you to take this action. As you do, everything you feel comes forward in an unplanned array of color and is further evidenced by your natural behavior and body language.

On the other hand, if you sing the song primarily for its musical values, you will be left to color the performance synthetically. This could take one of several forms. You might color the singing voice to show feeling, which is often called "emoting." Or you could perform a series of physical and emotional stances to go along with the sounds you're making. Or you might do what I call "being a fan of the song." This is when the song has affected you as a listener and you make your performance out of those feelings. Your personal response to the material might be a deep one; it might even be why you chose to sing it. But when you sing your feelings about it, you are merely being a fan of the song, a fan who knows how to sing.

Assuming you have learned the music well and dealt effectively with any vocal challenges a song may present you, the music will be there. It is a misunderstanding of your job as a singing actor to think of the words as a vehicle for the sounds you're making. You can sing your songs with just as much musical fidelity and bring them vividly to life by singing the words.

Now, please read these lines aloud.

My heart is so full of you
So full of you
There is no room
For anything more there

This is the first verse of a song by Frank Loesser, from a score that in itself offers us a master class in musical theater. Your spoken version of these lines was probably not all that different from your reading of the "Millwork" lyric. But looking at the score below, we see a song that is anything but conversational.

Please read or otherwise familiarize yourself with this fragment.

"My Heart Is So Full of You"
From "The Most Happy Fella" (1956)
Music & Lyrics by Frank Loesser

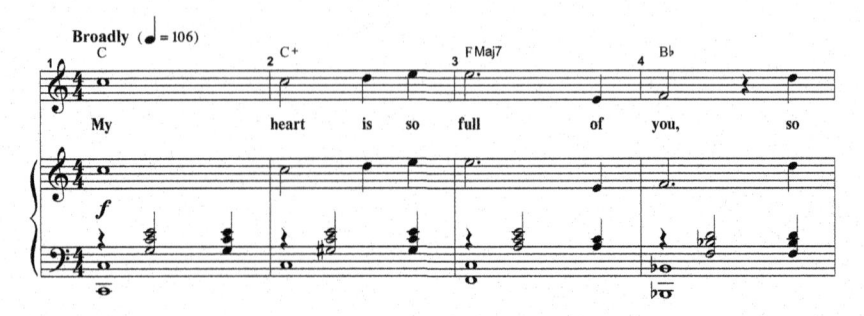

The conversational style of "Millwork" made singing the words a completely natural thing to do. Here, the length of the notes and the operatic style of the writing seem to suggest the opposite.

So yes, you will need to plan where to breathe and to be aware of how much breath you need and use. And yes, you would do well to pay attention to the vowels you are employing.

But as long as you *have* the necessary breath, you can think of these long notes as *sustaining the feeling*, not just the sound. And expressing the feeling to the other person is the action of the song. The music itself sounds like something that is overflowing the vessel in which it's held. The "something" is love, and the "vessel" is your heart. You have felt this feeling, and this wonderful music gives you the chance to express it in a song. But if you live primarily in the music, you can end up "swimming" in that feeling, rather than expressing it. This, in turn, can inadvertently make the song about *you* ("I'm feeling so much") instead of it being about the person you love ("This is what I feel for you").

If you fully explore both the opportunities and the responsibilities of the music, and practice it until you get it into your voice and body, the music will *be* there. The scene, however, will be found in the words.

Learning the Music

With existing musical theater material (from shows that have already been produced), it's best to learn songs from the original published sheet music or the original printed score. If you learn a song from a recording or video of another actor, you are learning the performance, not just the song. And though vocal performances on original cast recordings tend to be quite faithful to the written music, you are still learning how the other singer sounds.

At odds with this, there may be times when the people casting replacements for a show or those casting future productions may actually *want* you to sound like the original actor. But whether they say it or not, they also want you to surprise them and to illuminate the material by bringing it fully to life. These are difficult aims to juggle when learning a song, so it's best to start with what's on the page, without being unduly swayed by how the original actor sounded.

For *new* musicals, you are often given songs or pieces of songs from the show for auditions. This practice is common during the callback stage but seems to be gaining popularity for first auditions as well.

Along with the written music, you may be sent a digital recording of the melody and accompaniment to help you learn the music, and possibly a second recording of just the accompaniment, to rehearse with for your audition. If you are not given these additional materials, I strongly recommend paying a professional accompanist to provide them for you.

When you've been cast in a workshop or production of a musical, the rehearsal process will usually begin with the musical director teaching the score to the company. Being able to sight-read is always a plus for the singing actor, but in most cases, learning by ear is perfectly acceptable, as long as you are confident and relatively quick in that process. If you learn slowly by ear, you are disadvantaging yourself by not learning to read music. Some actors use a combination of eye and ear in their learning process, and I often find that the extra concentration involved in relying at least partially on the ear can help actors get the music more completely in their bodies as they're learning it.

With standards (classic songs that have enjoyed great popularity over the years and been widely recorded), one should *always* use the original sheet music or score. These songs have been interpreted in countless ways, and often those interpretations will include melodic, rhythmic, and even lyric variations that speak as much of the singer as the song. Further complicating matters, the songs are sometimes then republished in editions that include a singer's particular variations, so make sure to buy the true original.

Since the mid-to-late 60s, rock and pop songs have more often than not been written by the singer or group that recorded them, or in collaboration with them. In these cases, the recording *is* the song, and the printed music reflects this by being a representation of the recorded performance. Even so, the printed music is still a preferable learning tool because learning from a recording can lead to vocal imitation. But then, vocal imitation may be just what's called for with certain shows. So, it's important to know when this is the aim and when it's not.

In all of the above situations, I would recommend learning your songs with the help of a professional accompanist, unless you are an accomplished musician yourself.

But isn't this supposed to be a book about acting? Why are we talking about how to learn music? Because you can't really act a song until you know it.

Rhythm

The rhythms of your song's melody line did not fall onto the page accidentally. They are part of the writing, and they are a valuable tool, a vehicle for moving forward, and for *bringing* forward everything you feel as you take action. And yet, this is the element of the music most likely

60　ABOUT MUSIC

to be handled casually by the actor. Crisp, accurate use of the written rhythms will not limit you; it will propel you and allow you to fly as you jump off the cliff.

To illustrate the importance of being rhythmically specific in your singing, I'll repeat just the melody and lyrics of the two music samples we started this chapter with, so we can study them for their rhythmic values.

"Millwork"
Music & Lyrics by James Taylor

[Musical notation with lyrics:]

Grand-dad was a sai - lor, and he blew in off the wa - ter. My fa - ther was a far - mer, and I his on - ly daugh - ter. I took up with a no - good mill - work - in' man from Mas - sa - chu - setts, who died from too much whis - key and leaves me these three fa - ces to feed.

Notice how each musical phrase has its greatest weight on the downbeat of a measure. The weight and specificity of these downbeats have great power, but that power will only be there for you if you use it. If you don't, the power itself will cease to exist.

Next, notice how phrases 1,2,3,4 and 6 have a near symmetry and that they all end in two-syllable words on the same rhythm: "sailor / water / farmer / daughter / whiskey." These rhythms create a pattern that then sets apart the two phrases that are different. These are number 5 ("I took up with a no-good millworkin' man from Massachusetts") and number 7 ("and leaves me these three faces to feed").

Obviously, these two lines are longer (four measures instead of two), but there are *other* differences within these lines that have to do with rhythm, differences that affect the very substance of the story.

The difference in phrase 5 is that, as it develops, it abandons the basic rhythmic cadence of all the other lines, to create an inelegant spill of detail and feeling. The character is unable to keep to the symmetry of those other lines because of what she feels when talking about the man. She blames herself for choosing him, and she blames him for everything he was and wasn't.

As for phrase 7, it is unlike all the other lines because it ends in a single syllable instead of two. It does this to express that this is indeed an ending: to the verse, to the woman's youth, and to any chance she ever had of getting out of the mill.

I've been using words like "weight," "importance," "blame," and "ending" in this discussion. This could make you think that the telling of this story should be weighty or dark. Quite the contrary, the song has the matter-of-fact, unadorned quality of a folk song because the character has been worn down by her work and her life and because she is not one to make a fuss.

How, then, can this song command the stage when the character is exhausted and profoundly humble? It does so through the woman's great inner strength and through the tautness and power of the rhythms.

Being one of the composers of "Working," I was there during an early workshop of the show, the day Robin Lamont first sang "Millwork." That day, she sang the rhythms exactly as they appear on the page. And a year later, when we opened on Broadway, she sang the same rhythms because the rhythms *are* the song, and they allow the power of the story and the riches of the actor's performance to come forward.

"My Heart Is So Full of You"
Music & Lyrics by Frank Loesser

[Sheet music: Measures 1–11 with lyrics "My heart is so full of you, so full of you, there is no room for a-ny-thing more there."]

Analyzing the sung rhythms of "My Heart Is So Full of You," we again see the force of the downbeats. Nine of the eleven measures in this first verse begin with a note on the downbeat of a measure. And just look at how much those syllables weigh and the role they play in what's being said.

Also of note is how square the vocal rhythms are throughout this verse. All those whole notes, half notes, dotted halves and quarters show an insistence and a certainty about what is being said, just as all the syncopations in a song like "Something's Coming" reveal a lack of certainty.

The rhythmic values of measures 7 and 9 are particularly interesting. If you compare beats 2, 3, and 4 of those two measures, you can see how the squareness and solidity of those three quarter notes in bar 7 set up the rhythmic variation in bar 9. That triplet in bar 9 is the first thing in the song that hasn't sat firmly on one of the four beats in a measure. What does that feel like? What does it mean?

Sing measures 7 through 11 and you'll see. If you sing the rhythms precisely as written, the effort involved in equally dividing three notes into two beats (in the triplet in measure 9) gives you a distinct pleasure. Or is it pain? Or is it so beautiful that it hurts? It also feels like you're somehow out of control, as if you were *falling*. But those three notes are *ascending*.

How can you be out of control, falling, and ascending all at once? Perhaps it's the "overflowing of the vessel" I spoke of earlier in this chapter.

The rhythmic values of all your songs were put there on purpose, and they can be an extraordinary vehicle for you in your acting. All you need to do is *use* them.

Volume & Dynamics

I believe that the deliberate use of dynamics is for groups: ensembles, choruses, and choirs. When I hear a soloist consciously making a crescendo, decrescendo, or other volume-related effect, I can't help but think of the other person, the vocal coach or musical director who told the actor to do that. I have great respect for these professionals. They are of vital importance in our lives and our work. But when volume is decided upon, exclusive of acting, it is just another way of using the voice to *replicate* feeling. If you are contouring sound to represent feeling, you cannot also be fully engaged in your scene, because the two activities pull in opposite directions.

But even without anyone else's input, there's a common misconception that many actors have about the use of dynamics, which is that songs need to be given a build by having the singer start out softly. Accompaniments will often start in a spare manner and have detail and volume added as the song continues. But for the actor, the actions you take have *energy*, and if you simply replace the word *volume* with the word *energy* in how you think about singing, all such misconceptions about volume fall away.

For me, the single biggest thing we do in a song is break the silence. Going from nothing to something is a huge occurrence. That doesn't mean we should decide to sing the first line of a song loudly. Whatever the size of the sound, it will occur naturally as a product of energy, action, and breath.

Let's say you've decided to leave a marriage. Walking out the door with a suitcase will indeed be a "big" moment. But just as big, if not bigger, is daring to say: "We have to talk." If you ever find yourself in this position, I can assure you that you won't be thinking about volume as you broach the subject.

Songs don't start small, nor do they start big. They simply start, and they *wouldn't* start if what was being said wasn't important. But what if the song is playful and light; for instance, "When I'm 64" (Lennon and McCartney) or "Orange Colored Sky" (Milton DeLugg and Willie Stein)? My point remains: you wouldn't be breaking the silence to say even these light, playful things if what was being said didn't matter.

I've had any number of students tell me that someone along the way told them they sing "too loud." This comment may have come from a teacher, a fellow actor, an agent, a casting director, anyone really. Hearing this will usually result in the actor becoming self-conscious and trying to sing with less volume, but doing this will only make you invisible.

Here's what I know. You are in a vulnerable profession, one in which you might try all kinds of things to feel less vulnerable. If you have a big voice, you may have unwittingly used it to arm and protect yourself. You might think that you're just trying to showcase one of your strengths (your big voice), but if all that sound isn't backed up by true emotion and purpose, it can push us away. If it comes from feeling and action, no amount of volume is too much. Once again, it's not about the size of the sound, it's about acting.

Pitch

It's hard to excel at anything in life when you're worried about your very ability to do it. Whatever the task is, "trying not to fail" will lead to an effortful, distracted performance, or to failure itself. Singing on pitch is no exception. If you've ever been told you have an issue with pitch or have ever actually *had* an issue with it, you may be prone to this sort of self-defeating behavior.

It's possible that there are flaws in how you use your breath or your voice that affect the pitch, but these can be successfully dealt with in your vocal studies, without isolating pitch as a separate concern. Or it's possible you once had a problem with one note, in one song, and the way it was dealt with caused you to "get in your head" about this aspect of singing.

I believe that good pitch is like breathing, that nature has provided us with the equipment and the ability to hear and make pitch. But if you ever struggle in this area, I can offer you the following insights.

The pitch is always at eye level. It's not on the ceiling, or the floor, or anywhere in-between, except right in front of your eyes. Of course, the melody moves up and down, but you do not need to reach up to it or dip down to it.

At the same time, the pitch is not some thin thread that is difficult to find and maintain. Think of it vertically, and picture the center of the pitch as having a bit of height, say three or four inches. Looked at this way, the center of the pitch is roomy; it is impossible to miss, and it is there for you to live in and enjoy.

Other than these visual images, if you concern yourself with what you're saying and why, every aspect of your singing will improve, including *this* one.

Vanity

Let's say you're mid-song in a performance or audition and you've just sung the best, most perfect note you have ever produced. That's a good thing, right? Now, let's say you've just failed spectacularly on a particular note. I think we would all agree that's *not* a good thing. But here's what the two things have in common; *they're over.* So, do you really want to be in celebration or mourning for a note you've already sung, as you continue singing the song?

These two vastly different responses to your own singing are equally destructive to your performance. When you engage in either one of them, bad things happen. First of all, you are thinking about yourself, instead of what you're doing (note the title of this section). Secondly, you can't possibly still be acting, because you're celebrating or mourning.

Then, you will probably become aware of this and realize you have just driven the last mile without looking at the road. This will no doubt scare you. Panicked, you will then start to pretend. If the song is happy, you will be *very* happy. If the song is sad, angry, romantic, whatever, that's what you'll pretend to be. All the while, you will continue to harbor thoughts of the triumph or tragedy of the now famous note.

Here's how to avoid all of this. If you are truly engaged in your scene/song, you are less likely to be distracted in the first place. But if you do become distracted by this or anything else, it is possible to re-up to your action. This is a natural act, something we do in life all the time, when we're thrown off course by an irrelevant event or stray thought.

It is not possible to re-up to preparation because, by definition, preparation is over by the time the song begins. But if indeed you've been successfully engaged in your action and you're somehow pulled away from it, you can find your way back to that action. This takes practice, of course, but so does everything else that's worth learning.

Acapella

There are situations in which you may be asked to sing without accompaniment. Obviously, when auditioning for a musical that is to be performed acapella, you will be asked to show this skill.

Agents will occasionally ask actors to sing acapella for them. This doesn't mean they are looking for clients who are accomplished at this. It means that while you are in their office being interviewed, they decide they would like to hear your singing voice. This most often happens if you have musicals on your resume and if the agent is interested in you.

Regional theaters and other not-for-profits may sometimes have you sing without accompaniment if they are not accustomed to doing musicals. This may also occur with directors who are new to musical theater, or with hybrid projects, where the role of music is limited or yet to be defined.

In all of these situations, you will be making music by yourself. So, there are components of the music, such as pace and key, for which you're used to having support, that are now solely your responsibility. These two aspects of the music are the things most likely to be handled unsuccessfully by the actor when singing acapella.

To set a tempo, hear it in your head before you begin singing. If the melody has phrases or measures that have more activity than others, it's better to choose these more active passages for setting your tempo. For instance, if you were about to sing "My Heart Is So Full of You," the phrase that says "there is no room" might be more useful for setting a tempo for yourself than the title phrase. This is how conductors often work. Before they raise their baton or their head to conduct the musicians, they hear and feel the tempo.

For actors, the tendency when setting a tempo is to rush, due to feeling heightened or anxious in this situation. Once again, a deep breath is the best remedy. Take a breath, hear the music in your head, and trust yourself.

Once you hear the tempo and begin singing, you need to then hold that tempo. The biggest challenges to holding your tempo are in the long notes and the spaces. When actors are not experienced with acapella, they will very often shorten the length of the sustains and shorten the spaces between phrases. This mars your performance by making the pace erratic and formless.

I would recommend that you begin your rehearsal process with the aid of a metronome or a drum machine of some sort. You'll be amazed how frequently you are tempted to pull ahead of the tempo. After a while, remove this element from your rehearsals and you will fare far better than if you had never used it.

Staying true to your starting key is just as important. Many songs have internal key changes, but those changes have a relationship to the initial key. So, whether your song stays in one key or moves around, you need to remain true to where you began. In your early rehearsals, use a keyboard or a cellphone app to check your pitch periodically throughout the song.

When you are about to audition an acapella song, you can get your starting pitch before entering the room or by playing a single note, if there's a piano in the room. Very often, singers can just pick the proper pitch out of the air (or at least one very close to it). This does not take perfect pitch. All it takes is knowing how certain pitches feel in your voice and trusting yourself to find them.

In singing for an agent in their office, the request is usually a casual one. This doesn't mean that you should necessarily treat the rudiments of singing acapella casually. It does mean, however, that the excellence of musicianship called for when auditioning for an acapella musical is not required here. The agent just wants to hear your voice.

In any of the above situations, you should choose a song your listeners are likely to know. This way, as you sing the melody, they will be filling in a lot of the missing harmonic information in their heads without even trying to. If they don't know the song, this won't happen.

Musical Paths

You are 31 years old and come to musical theater with fifteen years of classical vocal training. You have a master's degree in vocal performance from a top conservatory and have worked in opera and in the choruses of Golden Age musicals around the country. You want to play roles in both traditional and contemporary musicals and would like to work on Broadway.

After breaking the ice in our first two classes, with cuts of "Soliloquy" from "Carousel" (Rodgers and Hammerstein) and "You Should Be Loved" from "Side Show" (Henry Krieger and Bill Russell), you brought in "Over the Rainbow" from "The Wizard of Oz" (Arlen and Harburg). In those first two classes, I had introduced such ideas as "singing and speaking being more alike," and "not using dynamics as a stand-in for feeling."

But while you understood what I was attempting to guide you to, you responded by trying to *create* the vocal effects you thought I wanted, by using technical means. Specifically, in an effort to sound more conversational, you sang with less volume and artificially clipped the length of notes.

Something else surfaced in those early sessions, though. When talking about your life experience and the musical path that had led you here, you exhibited depth, humor, heart, humility, and more. None of this had been visible in your singing, because you had been trying to *make* qualities to go along with your vocal performances.

With "Over the Rainbow," you began in the same manner, but the simplicity of the song, and your comfort level from now being in your third class, gave us an opportunity to move forward.

I give you a chair and ask you to sit close, facing the class. "Tell us what's in your refrigerator," I say. You are surprised, which is not surprising. But once I'm able to convince you to take my request literally, you begin to tell us. There's a chicken dish you make enough of to last for three days, some Greek yogurt, raw string beans, frozen berries, almond milk, a jar of wheat germ and beer.

I ask you if this person, this guy who makes the chicken dish, can do your singing for you. You're not sure how. I tell you that I'm going to ask you to speak again, after which I'd like you to go directly into singing "Over the Rainbow," without altering your tone. I tell the accompanist to give you your starting note now, so you will have it when you need it, and not to play any intro when the song begins.

I then ask you where you first heard this song. You tell us about a living room floor in New Mexico, and a VCR, which you explain is "an ancient technology from an early civilization." "Let's go," I say.

And here's what we all get to see and hear: a man who is also a boy, a fine singer who has a story to tell, and someone revealing his true power by allowing us to see his softness. You have begun the work you had hoped to do, and even better, you know it.

Note: Why the refrigerator question? I might just as well have asked the student to describe his favorite pair of socks, and their history, or how to play chess. The point was to get him communicating, as himself, to us, about *anything*.

To accomplish the task of telling us what was in his refrigerator, he would have to truly engage in a thought process. He would have to see, in his mind's eye, the inside of his refrigerator and then translate the images he saw into words.

If he truly did this (which he did), he would have no choice but to be himself and to use his voice to actually communicate with us. This is what I wanted to guide him to in "Over the Rainbow." But he wasn't quite ready to make the leap and needed one more bit of help.

So, I left the world of the mundane (the refrigerator) and went to the heart (the living room floor). He would once again need to go through the realistic process of collecting imagery and finding the words to tell us about it. But two things would be different in this exercise. One, he would have the opportunity to go directly from speaking to singing. And two, if he was willing to truly engage in answering the question, he would already be in the fertile territory the song lives in: one's youth, one's hopes, and one's spirit.

*　*　*

You studied dance throughout your childhood and came to focus on ballet by age 10. You also sang in school choirs and played supporting roles in high school shows and community theater. You auditioned for and were accepted into a good university musical theater program, where from 18–21 you studied acting, singing, and dancing.

You did well in your acting classes freshman year but struggled somewhat after that. There were some truly excellent singers in your program, which caused you to believe you didn't sing well. You excelled in your dance studies, played dancing roles in musicals, and were the go-to person when your friends needed help with their own dancing.

Once in New York, at 22, you found your way to Studio 4R. In our early sessions, you showed yourself to be a solid actor, when engaged in your scene, and a nervous singer. When singing, most of your energy went into trying to make good sounds.

One day, you bring in "Bluebird" by Sara Bareilles. Instead of singing, I ask you to dance the song, no singing, while the accompanist plays the music. This, of course, is beautiful. Then I ask you to engage in a second exercise. This time, I'd like you to just stand still, feeling the music and thinking the words, as the accompanist plays. Then, you sing the song and are freer in your acting and singing than at any time in our work thus far.

I then ask what it had been like for you in college, when you would help your friends with their dancing. "It felt good." "Yes, but what did you notice about their dancing?" You think for a moment, then respond: "They were usually better than they thought, and they got in their own way." You don't immediately see the connection, but everyone else in class seems to instantly make the leap. Once you catch up, you laugh at yourself, always a useful thing to do.

It's not that this problem then miraculously went away. You had spent too much time believing in it. But you at least understood the nature of the problem and could see that it wasn't as much about singing as a sense of *inferiority* about singing. "Compare and despair," one of my students calls this. The profession breeds it. But, like any mindset that limits us, it can be cured.

Find the right vocal coach. Study voice. Take acting classes. Work on your skills and yourself. And stop defeating yourself by thinking that being good at one thing automatically means you aren't good at something else.

* * *

You went to theater camp each summer, a performing arts high school, and a 2-year musical theater conservatory in New York. An exceptional singer and a confident actor and dancer, you graduated at 20, after which you did a season of summer stock and a year-long, non-union tour, where you understudied the leading role. Upon returning to New York, you were in a workshop of a new musical, a handful of concerts for young composers, and a NYMF show (New York Musical Festival).

In your first 2 years out of school, you were constantly working and even making a good salary on the tour. Then, a year of nannying, more free concerts for composers, and coming in second for jobs.

You came to audit one of my classes with a friend from your summer stock days. And a month later, you auditioned for me. Your book of music was full and varied. Among the highlights, "Mama Who Bore Me" from "Spring Awakening" (Sater and Sheik), "The Light in the Piazza" (Guettel), "On the Steps of the Palace" from "Into the Woods" (Sondheim), "Glitter in the Air" (by Pink and Billy Mann), "On the Other Side of the Tracks" from "Little Me" (Coleman and Leigh), and "Itsy Bitsy Teenie Weenie Yellow Polka Dot Bikini" (a bubblegum pop song from 1960 by Paul Vance and Lee Pockriss). Your singing voice and technique were first-rate, but you confided in me that you had lost much of the confidence you had coming out of school.

We begin working together, and yes, the stated goal is for you to regain your confidence, but how taking this class can help you do that is multifaceted. The class offers you a safe place to work out, a community of talented actors who are truly supportive of one another, a chance to re-explore those useful songs in your book, some new ideas of songs you might look at, and a place to prepare for auditions.

But then there is the work itself, which for me is always about acting. Here are some notes I made during your first 2 classes. Until now, these scribblings were between me and my yellow legal pad. Now, they're in this book.

"Honestly engaged in her action, full of feeling, then starts to *pretend* the very thing she had genuinely felt. It's as if she is observing real behavior (her own) and then trying to mimic it. Also, when singing really impressive notes, she is taken out of the scene."

So, we work on strengthening the actions you take and staying engaged in them while allowing what you feel to flow and change as you go. As actors, the actions we take in our scenes will most often remain constant, even though we may use multiple tactics within a given action. But what we feel and experience is *never* constant. It is ever shifting, always alive.

Your recent loss of confidence may have exacerbated this tendency to augment your real behavior with synthetics, but it's also possible that this is what you've always done. Either way, it's solvable by improving and, in fact, simplifying your process, giving more attention to action and then trusting that you are enough.

Now for your loss of focus when letting loose vocally. You love to sing, and you're good at it. But "enjoying singing" is not an action and it can overshadow any real action you may be engaged in.

Again, like the first issue, this tendency to luxuriate in your singing, to the detriment of your acting, could be something you've always done, but as we discussed earlier in the chapter, being pleased (or displeased) with how you sound is nothing more than a distraction, and it disrupts the flow of your performance.

The heady act of singing can and should be coupled with the scene you're playing. Those fun-to-sing sustains in "My Heart Is So Full of You" are there to express love, and that lingering last note of "Something's Coming" is about who you are, where you are, and what you long for.

And those riffy last lines of "Defying Gravity" are a thrilling opportunity to express the character's defiance and ownership of her own power. Those notes are powerful, but coming from the larynx instead of your whole self, they are meaningless.

Oh, and the student gets her confidence back, and her first Broadway show.

* * *

You took piano lessons as a child, but never enjoyed it. As a psychology major in college, you joined an acapella group, singing tenor. Junior and senior years, you auditioned for and were cast in student-sponsored musicals, playing overweight guys who sing boisterously: Herman in "Sweet Charity," and Thenardier in "Les Misérables."

After college, you gave yourself a year to see how you might do as an actor in New York. You came to audition for me and brought the following songs: "I Love to Cry at Weddings" from "Sweet Charity" (Cy Coleman and Dorothy Fields), "Master of the House" from "Les Misérables" (Schonberg and Boublil) and "Sit Down, You're Rockin' the Boat" from "Guys and Dolls" (Loesser). Your audition revealed a false energy and a terrific voice.

As we get to know each other in class, I suggest some different kinds of songs for you to work on. Out in the world, you may very well be typecast for your body type, but typing yourself in this way will not help you become a good actor.

You learn music quickly (the piano lessons? the acapella group?), and you start to bring in a new song each week. You begin with "Love Who You Love" by Lynn Ahrens and Stephen Flaherty from "A Man of No Importance." As we go through the song multiple times, I give you different classmates to be your scene partner. For each new partner, I give you an invented reason they need to hear this and advise you to make the scene about *them*. One of the oddities of acting is that the more you make the scene about the other person, the more we see *you*. A personal analogy to this is that every now and then while teaching I'll have a random thought like "Gee, I wonder how to teach." The answer is always: "Concentrate on the student."

So, in this session, you begin to truly "act" for the first time because for the first time you're not putting on a show for us. You're trying to help the other person make their life better, by giving them permission to be themselves. And in the process, you get to be yourself, too.

Next up, "Pity the Child" from "Chess" (Tim Rice, Benny Andersson, and Bjorn Ulvaeus), then "New York State of Mind" (Billy Joel), then "Without a Song" (Vincent Youmans, Edward Eliscu, and Billy Rose), and on from there.

When you type yourself, you're saying: "This is all I am." The more you do this, the less we are drawn to you. We need to see your humanity, your true sense of humor, and your unique energy. By denuding yourself of *yourself*, in an effort to be castable, you become hollow.

* * *

By age 27, you had toured the world as a back-up singer for rock and pop acts. Prior to that, you had graduated as valedictorian of your class from a conservatory for straight acting in New York. You had tried to bring your singing skills and your acting skills together and had not been able to. You had never had a successful audition for a musical.

You began your work in class by singing eclectic contemporary musical theater pieces such as "Gainesville" from Randy Newman's "Faust," my song "The Picture in the Hall" from a musical play I wrote with Craig Lucas called "Three Postcards," and the end of "Meadowlark" from "The Baker's Wife" by Stephen Schwartz (starting at "and now I stand here starry-eyed and stormy . . .").

In these, you showed yourself to be a first-rate contemporary singer who labors somewhat to connect with her songs as scenes.

Then you bring in "Think" (by Aretha Franklin and Ted White) in which you are everything you are trying to be. We talk about why this song is different for you, from a song like "Meadowlark." First of all, you are thinking of the Aretha Franklin song in simpler terms. Yes, it's sort of a scene, in that you are singing to an ex in the song, and you relish venting your frustration and anger toward him in this way. But you're not really approaching the song as something theatrical, and you also feel very at home with this style of music. Whereas, with "Meadowlark," the plot of the musical makes you think you need to have a more complex way of coming at the song. But also, you feel out of your element with "this kind of song," and don't yet have a successful way of singing the high note near the end, on the word "past."

Luckily, you have just begun working with one of New York's best vocal coaches, and she will help you strengthen and broaden your vocal abilities while we work on acting together.

But for right now, before that vocal work has even begun, I ask you to simplify your scenario for the "Meadowlark" fragment, to just keep the personal reference you used the first time, about liberating yourself from a relationship that was holding you back, and to overlook, for the time being, that the high note toward the end may sound imperfect. Then, I ask you to simply approach the singing and the scene in the same visceral way you had approached "Think," the operative word being "visceral." You are excited by the challenge, but given your skills, it ends up not being much of a challenge at all. You make a leap, and then another. And, as if by magic, you start getting jobs.

* * *

So much is said about "types of songs," but very often, thinking of songs as types can lead to preconceptions that limit the actor. "I can't sing rock" / "I'm not funny" / "I'm no good at traditional musical theater" / "I hate this kind of song" / "I don't sound contemporary." But isn't this just another way of typing *yourself*?

5

TYPES OF SONGS

You will be asked to sing many different kinds of songs in your career, but the task of acting and singing them isn't really all that different from category to category. The genre of the song you've been given for an audition, class, production, or concert may be patently clear to you. Or, if you're doing the choosing yourself, you've no doubt chosen the song because it is the appropriate "type of song" for the occasion. But you don't then have to approach it as a "type."

I've known Sheldon Harnick for 40 years, and we've often talked about songwriting, but a couple of years ago, I had the opportunity to interview this master lyricist about his work, and he told me something that relates to what we're talking about. He had never felt quite at home writing "love songs," until he wrote the lyric for the title song of "She Loves Me." What excited him about the song was that for the first time he felt he was using his own authentic voice in a love song. To quote Sheldon:

"I remember when I wrote that lyric, I thought 'My God, that's really me. That's the way I feel and it's in the song now.'"

So once again, the process and the challenges of the writer resemble the process and the challenges the actor faces. As an actor, when thinking of a song as being of a particular type, there can be a temptation to act the type of song it is, rather than acting the song itself. This tendency increases when you believe yourself to not be as good at this genre as you are at others.

In this chapter, we'll look at a number of different types of songs and see how the principles we've been discussing in this book can be applied to these vastly different styles, all of them common types of songs actors are asked to bring to auditions or asked to sing in shows.

Note: This chapter is not meant to be an encyclopedic study of different styles of music and song. There are whole categories I will be leaving out, and within the ones I've chosen, there are numerous sub-genres I may make only a passing reference to. I say this to remind myself and the reader that even in this discussion of "types of songs," the focus will be on acting.

Contemporary Musical Theater

This is probably the most common type of song actors are asked to bring to auditions. I've recently used the term "Contemporary Musical Theater" myself, in casting breakdowns for a new show I've written, and yet the term is nebulous, at best.

Attempting to define it here, I came up with the following: "Any show that mixes elements of popular contemporary music with theater." Here's another try: "In 1968, 'Hair' (Galt MacDermott, Gerome Ragni, James Rado) successfully wed rock and theater for the first time. Then, in 1970, Hal Prince and Stephen Sondheim redefined musical theater with 'Company.' Contemporary Musical Theater is the result of these two events."

Not wholly satisfied with either of these definitions, I asked my friend Michael Hicks for his thoughts on the subject. Michael is one of the busiest and best audition accompanists in New York, so he's in rooms every day with different creative teams who are engaged in the act of making new musicals.

Here's Michael's definition: "Something that has been written within the lifetime of everyone behind the table, especially, but not exclusively, the writers."

In other words, the term is subjective. That sounds right, doesn't it? On any given day, in two neighboring rooms at Ripley-Grier or Pearl Studios, the question of what this genre might be is being answered in two entirely different ways.

This fits with what I've always done in class when a student has been asked to bring in a Contemporary Musical Theater song for a new show. We start with questions. "Have you heard the score?" "Has anyone in class heard it, or seen a workshop, or heard one of the songs in a concert?" "What do we know about the writers? Have we heard something else they've written?" "Do they have a website?" "Have you tried YouTube?"

Using any and all of these means, you will probably be able to get some idea of what kind of Contemporary Musical Theater you are auditioning for. Are we talking about "Waitress" or "Giant," "Ordinary Days" or "Assassins," "In the Heights" or "Hadestown," "Mean Girls," "The Color Purple," or "Rent?" Because they're all different, as are the hundreds of shows I didn't mention, and these differences would affect what you would choose to sing for a first audition.

But when it comes to acting, everything we've been talking about in this book so far is applicable to the entire crazy-quilt of authors and titles that make up this genre called Contemporary Musical Theater.

— Trusting yourself and your instincts
— Singing the words
— Using the rhythms
— Becoming the author
— Being specific in your preparations
— Playing action instead of qualities and attitudes
— Acting vs. performing

All of this applies to almost all of this sprawling genre, from "Hair" to "Hamilton," and beyond. "Almost," because there are a number of sub-genres within Contemporary Musical Theater for which these basic principles may need to be adapted somewhat.

Four Sub-genres

Comedy (with a Tilt)

There are musicals that are built on an entirely comedic foundation or premise, like "The Book of Mormon," "Avenue Q," and "Urinetown." Each of these has a specific comedic "tilt" to them that calls for some kind of artful mix of performing and acting. When shows of this style are at their very best, the distinctive off-kilter world of the show is evident in all aspects of the production. The most common mistake actors make when auditioning for (or even performing in) musicals of this kind is to approach the material with a generalized, heightened energy. By not regarding the individual comedic tilt of the show, you flatten it out, and regardless of how much energy you expend, your performance will not be successful.

I also believe, though, that *all* acting needs to have a reality base, including the acting of totally comedic shows. The characters may be cuckoo, and the quest they're engaged in may be absurd, but they need to believe totally in what they're doing. Their actions need to be plausible to themselves, in order to be funny to us.

Pop-Melodrama

"The Phantom of the Opera," "Les Misérables," "Miss Saigon," "Jekyll and Hyde" and others make up a pop-melodrama style of Contemporary Musical Theater. This phenomenally successful sub-genre is defined by an abundance of melody, rich story lines, and enormous "size." When shows of this kind are acted well, the performances are expansive and passionate, and the "size" is earned because it comes from inside the actors.

But that's the challenge, because if the size doesn't come from inside you, the show itself will still be enormous, and you will be left to match that size by filling out your performance with synthetics, such as physical and emotional posturing, vocal contouring, and bluster.

You can live in your character's shoes and fill them ably by playing your role with an expansive, motivated reality, and by not allowing yourself the convenience of artifice.

I spoke earlier of everything in "Sweeney Todd" being "times 100." That was a deliberate exaggeration, of course. But musicals themselves are often called "larger than life." I would say, instead, that they are "life at its largest," and this is never truer than in this pop-melodrama style of Contemporary Musical Theater.

Disney

Disney musicals are in a category of their own. In fact, actors are sometimes asked to bring a Disney song to a non-Disney audition precisely *because* they're in a category of their own.

The Disney scores are most certainly contemporary, but for the actor, playing roles in Disney musicals, and auditioning for those roles, can present something of the same challenge you might encounter when acting in Golden Age musicals. In both genres, the characters can tend to be drawn without ambiguity. They are either innocent or worldly, harmless or dangerous, serious or funny. And though the Disney heroines are all smart and have a fierce sense of independence (since Ashman and Menken first modernized the form with the animated film "The Little Mermaid"), when performed live, they still more closely resemble the traditional ingénues of the Golden Age than the young women we see in most musicals of the past 20–30 years.

As an acting teacher, I have found that Ariel, Belle and those that have followed can be brought more fully to life (exactly as written) by simply allowing them to have the complexity we know every young girl in the audience to have. And the same kind of thinking can be applied to all the princes, soldiers, fathers, friends, and villains we meet in these stories.

Jukebox

The term "Jukebox Musical" has a certain accuracy to it, in that all shows of this kind have scores made up of existing pop and rock songs. But there are differences in type and tone within this sub-genre, and those differences affect how to approach each given show as an actor.

"Mamma Mia!" (which opened on Broadway in 2001, after its 1999 London Premiere) is generally acknowledged to have pioneered the form. The songs of ABBA are used to tell the story of a young woman and her mother. The young woman has never met her father and is about to be married. She reads her mother's diary from 20 years ago, determines that one of three men could be her father, and surreptitiously invites all three to the wedding.

The ABBA songs are sung within the story (as in a traditional book-musical) and are positioned to be something the characters might say, feel, or do in the situations they're in. Having worked with numerous Donnas, Sophies and Skys, I have found that the key to acting the "Mamma Mia!" songs often lies more in the book than the lyrics. Since the songs weren't originally written to tell this story, there are moments in the show where the literal meaning of a lyric is less useful to the actor than the situation, the relationships, and the action. The enormous popularity of the ABBA songs certainly accounts for much of the show's great success, but the story and the book by Catherine Johnson are what make it actable.

In "Jersey Boys" (2005), the creators are up to something else entirely. The play tells the story of The Four Seasons, using the songs the 1960s rock and roll group made famous (most of them written by Bob Gaudio and Bob Crewe). Directed by Des McAnuff and choreographed by Sergio Trujillo, almost all the songs are "performed" as the group might have performed them back in the day, showing the evolution of the group in performance, as the book (by Marshall Brickman and Rick Elice) tells their story.

For first auditions, actors were often told to bring in an appropriate song of the period and to "simply sing it." As a teacher helping actors prepare for these auditions, I took this to mean: "Don't *act* your songs as you might in a typical audition, because in the play, the songs are *performed*."

But when auditioning, how do you "simply sing it?" Clearly, they don't want you to "act" your song, to try to connect with it as a scene.

And they also don't want you to "perform" your song in the stylized manner of The Four Seasons. But I know from experience that they also don't want actors being so casual about what they're doing that they don't "take stage" in some way.

Here's a device I have found that allows you to have purpose and energy without doing any of those things. Rehearse your "song of the period" with a couple of friends. Make up harmonies, sing as you would if this threesome or foursome was singing on a street corner in New Jersey. Then, gradually take away the friends, but keep the action. In that situation, you are *just singing the song*. But you, the actor, know what it is you're doing. And it's true to the period and the music, without being inappropriately *showy*.

To date, most Jukebox musicals have relied on one or both of these theatrical conventions, that of "Mamma Mia!" (in which the songs tell the story) or that of "Jersey Boys" (where the songs are largely sung "in performance," as the story is being told). The actor's task is markedly different from one to the other.

For instance, "Ain't Too Proud," which arrived in the 2018/2019 season, has the most in common with "Jersey Boys." It has the same director and choreographer and an equally distinctive catalogue in the music of The Temptations, the 1960s R&B group that in one form or another has been performing live ever since.

But for the actor, the single biggest element these two shows have in common is the stance from which most of the songs are sung. To act the songs in "Ain't Too Proud" (or in "Jersey Boys") is to perform them as part of a particular group, in a particular time and place, with choreographed moves, a distinctive musical blend and a performance style specific to the group and the era. *That's* the acting, and in both shows, this concept is vastly successful.

It's worth noting, though, that in both "Ain't Too Proud" and "Jersey Boys," there are several songs sung by the characters *within* the story, as in "Mamma Mia!," and that this "traditional" musical theater stance is used to one degree or another in almost all Jukebox musicals, including "Motown," "On Your Feet!," "The Cher Show," "Summer," "Tina," and a growing list of others.

I find "Beautiful," (which opened in 2014) interesting because it uses a number of different conventions, and it succeeds so well because under the direction of Marc Bruni, the actors always know which of these conventions is operative at any given moment. The show, with book by Douglas McGrath, and choreography by Josh Prince, tells the story of songwriter Carole King (with songs by King, Gerry Goffin, Barry Mann, Cynthia Weil, and others).

The different stances from which the songs are sung include young rock and roll writers in the 50s and 60s auditioning their songs for a music publisher, various singing groups of the era in recording sessions or in live performances, and Carole King as we know her from her iconic 1971 album, "Tapestry."

The "audition" stance is used to great effect in "Beautiful." This is a real situation in songwriters' lives, and what makes it unique is that as songwriters, we always care more about what people think of the song than what they think of the performance. This is the opposite of what actors are used to experiencing at auditions, and it can be freeing and instructive for you to live in this opposing reality.

The "audition" stance was also used early in "Jersey Boys," when Bob Gaudio auditioned to join the group, by singing and playing an early song of his called "Cry for Me." I worked on this moment often in class, and what always made the scene feel true was the notion that in Bob's mind, *he* was auditioning *them*. He knew he was good. Who were *these* guys?

Knowing what you're *doing* at each moment in each of these shows, from what perspective or for what purpose you are singing the songs, allows you to act these roles with complexity and beauty.

One of the most striking moments in "Beautiful" is when Carole is performing live in the "Tapestry" period. There had been many "performance" scenes in the show as there are in almost all shows of this genre, and they had been given the kind of sheen and artificiality appropriate to each moment.

But when Carole is performing in the "Tapestry" period, she isn't "performing" at all. Jessie Mueller, and those who followed her in the role (a number of them students of mine), have sounded like Carole King to some degree, but capturing her essence seems to have been the real aim here. The character had come to be at home with herself by this time in her life. So, in performance, she simply means what she is saying, and the music is coming from her whole body.

"Jagged Little Pill," which arrived in the 2019–2020 season, uses the traditional book-musical form of "Mamma Mia!" but represents a major leap forward for this genre. It has an up-to-the-minute, contemporary story and an exceptional book by Diablo Cody that uses the intense songs of Alanis Morissette in such an artful way that they seem to have been written for this occasion. Directed by Diane Paulus and choreographed by Sidi Larbi Cherkaoui, "Jagged Little Pill" marks a real advancement for this often-glossy sub-genre and, as a result, the roles in this show can be acted as though you were in any other serious, contemporary musical.

I have gone on at length about this type of Contemporary Musical Theater because it is such a prevalent style right now in the theater, and there is not *one* type of Jukebox musical; there are many. You will be auditioning for these shows, and acting in them, and it's important to know in each case what the rules are and what conceptual stance or stances you are acting the songs from.

Traditional Musical Theater

There are various opinions about when the "Golden Age of Musical Theater" began, with some historians believing it began in the 1920s, when Rodgers and Hart, the Gershwins, Cole Porter, and Irving Berlin offered the world a new show every season or two. But most say it began in 1943, when Rodgers and Hammerstein revolutionized the form with "Oklahoma!" There is little disagreement, however, about when the Golden Age ended, with the late 1960s marking the close of the era.

The pre-"Oklahoma" musicals gave us many of the world's greatest and most enduring songs. These choice songs are often referred to as "standards," and collectively, they make up much of what is called "The Great American Songbook." But the storylines and characters in the pre-"Oklahoma" shows tended to be frivolous and cliché-ridden. With "Oklahoma!," Hammerstein treated the book of the musical as a play and demanded that the songs move the story forward. These advances were radical and, as a genre, musical theater never looked back.

So, for the sake of our discussion, let's say that Traditional Musical Theater began with "Oklahoma!" and ended with the arrival of "Hair" in 1968, and that when you are asked to sing a traditional musical theater song, this is most likely the period being referred to.

Most traditional musical theater productions you audition for, or appear in, will be more or less faithful to the original intent of the show. Daniel Fish's revisionist 2019 production of "Oklahoma!" is an exception because it aimed at, and succeeded in, turning the show on its ear. It challenged everything from the genre this musical ushered in, to the founding of the state of Oklahoma and, by extension, America itself.

More commonly, though, when Golden Age musicals are produced, they stay closer to the originals. Even when certain elements are rethought, as in Trevor Nunn's 1998 London production of "Oklahoma!" (seen on Broadway in 2002) – where Laurey started out as a farm-girl in overalls instead of the classic Golden-Age ingénue we usually see – the heart, soul, and spirit of the shows remain intact.

Chances are you are more accustomed to auditioning for, and acting in, contemporary musicals than traditional. This is one reason the traditional shows may seem somewhat foreign to you.

Another reason is that the moral dictates of the day led to gender and character stereotyping in many of the Golden Age shows that can make acting in them challenging.

For instance, a woman's sexual history seems to be a defining characteristic in many of the era's female roles. Laurey in "Oklahoma!," Fiona in "Brigadoon," Sarah Brown in "Guys and Dolls," Marian Paroo in "The Music Man," and scores of others are defined in large part by the fact that they are virgins, and their stories revolve a great deal around whether, and with whom, that status will change. Conversely, in the first three of these musicals, Ado Annie, Meg Brockie, and Adelaide have all been sexually active and are all presented as comedic characters. And in "The Music Man," while there is no "promiscuous" secondary female character, Harold Hill sings of his preference for these "sadder-but-wiser girls."

The musicals cited above are classics, with "Guys and Dolls" and "The Music Man" being among my all-time favorites, but this oversimplification of female characters being either inexperienced or loose, serious or funny, can be misleading and limiting to the actor.

I've known Kelli O'Hara since 2001 when she played Susan, the young female lead in "Sweet Smell of Success," for which I wrote the lyrics (music by Marvin Hamlisch, book by John Guare).

Since then, I have watched with much pleasure and no surprise as Kelli has become one of the great leading ladies of musical theater.

When she was playing Nellie Forbush in "South Pacific" at Lincoln Center, we had a conversation about her performance, and she told me that she and director Bartlett Sher had decided that Nellie was not inexperienced with men before her relationship with Emile. So, while this character's sunny spirit and bright worldview were accurately described in "Cockeyed Optimist" and "I'm In Love with a Wonderful Guy," this did not mean that Nellie was "innocent of life." Her optimistic outlook needn't mean that she's "perky" or "plucky." She can be life-loving and full of hope.

Looking at some emblematic male roles of the era, Frank Butler in "Annie Get Your Gun," is a champion sharp-shooter; Billy Bigelow is a charismatic carousel barker; Sky Masterson is a slick, high-rolling gambler; Sid Sorokin in "The Pajama Game" is a cocky factory foreman; and Lancelot in "Camelot" is a Knight of the Round Table. Five among dozens of men in traditional musicals who hit bulls' eyes, run the rides, win the bets, give the orders, and come out on top when jousting.

And every one of them has had a world of experience with women. Billy Bigelow even dreams of teaching his future son how to be a womanizer, like himself. But when he dreams of having a daughter, he wants to *protect* her from such men.

The gender clichés of the day are anchored by the bedrock double standard that men could be sexually active before marriage but women could not. And these clichés are a trap for the actor because they can cause women to play some false idea of what it is to be female and men to pretend at a type of maleness that is equally cartoonish.

The answer to all of this is to play each character as a person, a person who has a particular history, a specific set of strengths and weaknesses, and who is engaged in action from scene to scene.

Some of your character's history is written in the play, but much of it is added as you explore your role, asking questions about who you are, where you've been, and where you think you're headed. Among other things, this sort of biographical work can teach you how to inhabit your character physically; how they hold themselves and how they move. It's also useful to research the time and place in which your character lived (or might have lived) to help you avoid playing them as if they existed only in the Golden Age of Musical Theater.

"West Side Story" came along in 1957 and was a total anomaly. With a book by Arthur Laurents, music by Leonard Bernstein, lyrics by Stephen Sondheim, and direction and choreography by Jerome Robbins, this show broke old rules and new ground. Lost among the show's many innovations, there was an unmarried couple (Bernardo and Anita) with a healthy sex life, who were neither a joke nor a pair of sinners. And when the female lead (Maria) lost her virginity to Tony, the life and death problems that ensued had little to do with that fact.

In 1959, "Gypsy" (Laurents, Sondheim, and Robbins, this time with composer Jule Styne) gave us a leading female character who manipulated and controlled everyone in her sphere, until her "quiet" daughter, Louise, found an even greater power and became Gypsy Rose Lee. The men in "Gypsy" were no match for the power of either of these women.

Then came the 1960s, the birth-control pill, and the beginning of the "Sexual Revolution." In 1962, "No Strings" (music and lyrics by Richard Rodgers, book by Samuel Taylor) showed us a world of globe-trotting grown-ups who made no apologies about the sex they had or the lives they led.

In 1964's "Fiddler on the Roof" (book by Joe Stein, music by Jerry Bock, lyrics by Sheldon Harnick, direction and choreography by Jerome Robbins), three of Tevye's daughters got married, and their obvious virginity was never in question, nor was it of any great consequence. What mattered in "Fiddler" was the daughters' choice of husbands and the fact that they did the choosing for themselves, thereby breaking with tradition.

The same year, "Golden Boy" (book by Clifford Odets and William Gibson, music by Charles Strouse, lyrics by Lee Adams) gave us a cast of contemporary characters in a contemporary world, with the morality of the Golden Age nowhere to be seen.

In fact, by the mid-60s, the sexual revolution had begun to make the gender stereotypes of the traditional era feel antiquated and as false as they perhaps always had been.

"Cabaret" in 1966 (book by Joe Masteroff, music by John Kander, lyrics by Fred Ebb, direction by Hal Prince), "Hair" in 1968, and "Company" in 1970 completed this sometimes-uncomfortable transition from Traditional to Contemporary Musical Theater.

Note: There is a video on YouTube of Joshua Henry and Jessie Mueller in a recording studio doing the "If I Loved You" scene from Jack O'Brien's 2018 production of "Carousel." Please watch it.

This is how great traditional musical theater can be. There is no posturing, no underlining of the beats in the scene, no indicating of the characters' qualities. Billy and Julie are together in a moment of unexpected importance in their lives, and they simply have the courage to not run away from this inevitable coupling. In the video, these two fine actors are living the scene as if they were inventing it, while singing brilliantly.

Standards

These classic songs were written in the 1920s, 30s, 40s, and 50s for stage musicals, Hollywood films, the popular song market, and the world of jazz. For the actor, they are among the most versatile and actable songs you will ever find.

There is a consistently high level of craft and originality to standards, and because they were written to be the popular songs of their day, they tend to be more detachable from their original contexts than, say, contemporary musical theater songs.

As a guide, I will include some examples of titles and authors in this section, since student actors are sometimes unfamiliar with this genre.

The following is a *partial* list of composers and lyricists who wrote The Great American Songbook. Open an anthology of any of these writers and you will find multiple songs that would suit you beautifully for auditions, classes, and concerts.

Harold Arlen (composer, with Johnny Mercer and many other lyricists)
Irving Berlin (composer-lyricist)
Hoagy Carmichael (composer, with various lyricists)
Howard Dietz and Arthur Schwartz
Duke Ellington (composer, with various lyricists)
George and Ira Gershwin
Jerome Kern (composer, with Dorothy Fields and many other lyricists)
Johnny Mercer (lyricist, with Harold Arlen and many other composers)
Cole Porter
Richard Rodgers and Lorenz Hart
Harry Warren (composer, with various lyricists)

In a classroom setting, these songs can provide the student with a perfect piece of material to work out on that is free of external plot elements and full of open space in which to breathe and just *be*. In other words, there's nowhere to hide.

But who's looking to hide? Most actors, some of the time. It's an odd thing about us theatrical types. We crave the spotlight, but when we get it, we feel uncomfortably exposed. But *of course* we feel exposed; we're in a spotlight and there's an audience.

A big contemporary musical theater song with an aggressive energy, an active accompaniment, and some great high notes can make you feel powerful, but all that energy and activity are also providing you with cover.

Having nowhere to hide, as in a simple 32-bar ballad, can teach you how to tolerate that sense of exposure and to surrender to it, so you can do your best work.

For this and other reasons, I have always felt that standards make good audition songs. Occasionally, you may be asked to bring one to an audition. But more often, these pieces make a great second song or contrasting choice, precisely because they *are* simple and because they feature *you* instead of the song. I find when I'm behind the table and an actor is offering choices from their book as a possible second song, I will frequently choose the standard for this reason.

Another spot one of these songs may fill in your book is to be that one, all-purpose song that you love to sing and that provides us with a perfect introduction to you. At face value, the song may not seem right for *any* particular audition. This may just make it the right song for *all* of them.

Here are a few titles I've seen fill that spot in a student's book:

"When I Fall in Love" – Victor Young and Edward Heyman
"My Funny Valentine" – Rodgers and Hart
"When the Sun Comes Out" – Harold Arlen and Ted Koehler
"I Wish I Didn't Love You So" – Frank Loesser
"Without A Song" – Youmans, Eliscu, and Rose
"The Way You Look Tonight" – Jerome Kern and Dorothy Fields
"Million Dollar Baby" – Harry Warren, Mort Dixon, and Billy Rose
"Blame It on My Youth" – Oscar Levant and Edward Heyman

And when looking for up-tempo songs (also called up-tunes), there is no better place to look than the songs of this era. What I've always taken the term "up-tune" to mean is "a song with a tempo that is bright and a subject that points up." There are hundreds of songs written between 1920 and 1960 that unapologetically fit this description. Here are just a few examples:

"A Shine on Your Shoes" – Howard Dietz and Arthur Schwartz
"I'm Beginning to See the Light" – Duke Ellington, Johnny Hodges, Harry James, and Don George
"Zing, Went the Strings of My Heart" – James F. Hanley
"Goody Goody" – Johnny Mercer and Matty Malneck
"I've Got the World on a String" – Arlen and Koehler
"You've Got That Thing" – Porter
"Let's Misbehave" – Porter
"I Love a Piano" – Berlin
"They All Laughed" – George and Ira Gershwin
"I Wish I Were in Love Again" – Rodgers and Hart
"Orange Colored Sky" – Milton DeLugg and Willie Stein

When performing up-tunes, I will often see actors working too hard, as if the desired lightness can be achieved by effort. Of course, the opposite is true. The act of singing an up-tune should be like "tossing a pebble in a pond." Never a brick, always a pebble.

And once again, rhythm is a prime tool in this endeavor. The rhythms of your vocal line and the strong use of consonants will help your song bounce or leap or whatever playful action the music suggests. And feeling that music in your body, even while standing still, is a natural act and a pleasure. It feels good. The music creates that feeling.

Here are two exercises I've found that can help the actor find this lightness in their up-tunes.

1 – Rehearse the song while chewing gum. *Allow the gum to be more important than the song.* This will keep you from trying too hard. Then of course, remove the gum.
2 – Work with a scene partner. Facing your partner but not touching, make up dance steps as you sing and have your partner mirror them, the way a dance captain might work with a new cast member. No rehearsing or planning allowed.
2A – Do this same exercise again, switching roles, so now the scene partner is making up steps and you are mirroring, as you sing. Don't be concerned that you may look foolish. You *will* look foolish and you will just have to surrender to it. And that surrender will allow the buoyancy of the song to be there.

Fresh on the heels of those exercises, remove the partner and the dancing and keep the buoyancy.

Note: Standards (both ballad and up-tune) often have introductory verses that precede the body of the song. As a student of songwriting and a lover of songs, I find these verses fascinating and very useful for concerts and recordings. But for audition purposes, it's usually best to just sing the refrain.

For instance, when we looked at Irving Berlin's song, "What'll I Do?" in Chapter 2, I had us work without the introductory verse for a number of reasons. First of all, the refrain is brilliantly actable, while the verse is less so. Secondly, the use of language and the musical style of the refrain are timeless, while the verse music and lyric both seem to speak of the 1920s.

So, for audition purposes, if you were to use both parts of this song, you would, in essence, be singing two songs, and the second one is superior to the first. So, why not just sing the better song?

But even in those cases where the verse is as distinctive as the refrain (for example: "All the Things You Are" by Kern and Hammerstein; "They Can't Take Away From Me" by the Gershwins; "I Get a Kick Out of You" by Cole Porter; and many, many others), I still think you're usually better off without the verse for auditions.

Also, when your audition songs have brevity, you are more likely to be asked to sing another.

Rock and Pop

In Chapter 4, I made reference to a student who was initially more invested when singing the R&B song "Think" than she was in her cut of the contemporary musical theater song "Meadowlark." While acknowledging that this student generally felt more at home with rock than she did with theater songs, I think there may have been something else in play here.

I've spoken at length about rhythm and how the rhythms of any song are a valuable tool for bringing forward everything you feel as you take action. Well, this aspect of your songs can be more readily apparent and easier to access in rock and pop, perhaps because these songs were born with drums in them, or perhaps because rock itself is a visceral genre.

In the song "Think," the emotion of the situation could conceivably make the character hit something or *someone*. But that same emotion might cause her to sing, and it does. The reason to physically lash out and the reason to sing are one and the same in this case. And the rhythms of the song are expressive of that.

So, however it occurred, the earthy, colloquial quality of "Think" helped my student understand and tap into the passions that were waiting to be expressed in "Meadowlark."

On the flip side, we see so much "performing" of rock songs by the original artists that quite intentionally has more to do with attitude than acting. Added to that, the "music video" has become as important an expression of the song as the audio recording or the writing itself. And as a separate art form, music videos make abundant use of additional elements that are not part of the song itself, such as locations, costumes, staging, story visualization, surreal imagery, and quick cutting from visual to visual.

In an audition room, there's nothing but you, the writing, and a piano. So, once again, the job of inhabiting the song effectively comes back to the basics of your approach to the song, your preparation, and your action. So, just as the visceral quality of rock can be invaluable when applied to our theater songs, the principles of acting are of great importance as we bring our rock and pop songs to the theater.

Vowel sounds are sometimes altered by the originating artists of rock and pop songs. For instance, you might hear the word "you" pronounced as "yo," or the word "I" pronounced as "Ah." In an audition room, emulating such idiosyncrasies, to the degree that they are accentuated in the rock world, can seem false or imitative.

An easy answer to this is to spend some of your rehearsal time pronouncing the words as you yourself might say them. That way, if you do gravitate back to the original singer's idiosyncrasies, you will probably arrive somewhere between the two pronunciations.

Riffing can be exciting but is used rather selectively in theater, because when overused, it can tend to pull focus away from what is being said. If you are called upon to riff, I know of only two ways to do it successfully. One is to be a person who has an innate sense of music and harmony, and the vocal flexibility to be able to express it in improvisational singing. Ray Charles would be my dictionary definition of this. The other way is to structure a riff deliberately and to practice it until it feels like second nature. There's no shame in this. Not everyone is Ray Charles.

Confusion can occur when you fit in the second category but you think you need to fit into the first. This can lead to sloppy riffing and an overall lack of musicality. Or it can occur when you assume this sort of musical invention is called for in a given show, but it isn't.

In theater music, a riff will sometimes be notated as it is at the end of "Defying Gravity." This means it is now part of the song. The notated riff is not necessarily an invitation to invent further ornaments. Then again, it *may* be. The composer and the musical director will have that answer, and it may differ from show to show.

In any case, riffing should never be about "you riffing." It's an extension of what you're feeling and doing.

Funny Songs

There are very few songs that actually make people laugh. There are songs that are built on a surprising, comedic idea, and those that have good jokes in them, but those things only tend to make us laugh the first couple of times we hear a song. What ends up being funny in performance is spontaneity, behavior, and under it all, truth.

When students have asked me to recommend funny songs for them, I have always felt it was something of a trick question, because I know that most often what will make the material funny is not the song but the person singing it.

So, I'm going to talk about a handful of specific performances I've seen in class over the years that have made me and the class laugh, and try to explore *why* they were funny, to see if we can get a handle on this slippery subject.

* * *

Hannah Shankman sang "Arabian Nights" from "Aladdin" (Howard Ashman and Alan Menken) before the stage version came along. Ashman's lyric has a sharp, sly wit to it, but what made us all laugh in class (on multiple occasions) was the snake-charmy seriousness with which Hannah wove her exotic tale.

What was funny – Ashman's witty lyric and Hannah's total commitment to her approach and her story.

Note: After successfully using this comic audition piece a number of times, Hannah shrewdly saw a greater versatility in it. By changing her approach, she was able to use the song to audition for, and book a role in, the 2014 Broadway revival of "Side Show."

* * *

D.B. Bonds (now a director and acting teacher) used a song called "Fanny Pack" (Ben Cohn and Sean McDaniel) to get cast in the First National Tour of "Dirty Rotten Scoundrels." This is a truly preposterous song in which the singer just *loves* his fanny pack and sings to it. D.B. was so genuinely excited about his love object that each new, ludicrous idea was a genuine discovery.

What was funny – the silly lyric and the actor's crazed excitement, which threatened to overwhelm him but which he somehow kept contained.

* * *

Lindsay Northen brought in a very funny song by Marcy Heisler and Zina Goldrich called "Compromise." In the song, a young woman is telling us about her "boyfriend," who from what we can see (but she can't) has little to no interest in her. Meanwhile, she is loaning him money, picking up his dry-cleaning, and giving us advice about love and relationships, because now "she really knows." The song is funny and so is Lindsay, but it took us a couple of sessions to find the right approach.

We came to realize that we had both been thinking of the character as stupid, which was causing us to condescend to her. This is never a good idea. So, I suggested that Lindsay find a real person in her life who might do and say these kinds of things. She arrived at someone she had once sat near in an ensemble dressing room. There was constant chatter from the castmate's direction about this man or that man and how much she was learning about life and love. The woman thought of her stories and insights as smart and instructive. In fact, she thought of *herself* as smart.

Two references from earlier in the book that relate to this: "Villains never know they're villains. In *their* story, they're the hero." And "Every character only knows what they know. Everything else, they *don't* know."

So, I asked Lindsay to simply *be* this other woman, and just like that, the song worked.

What was funny – Heisler's lyric is funny, and in Lindsay's hands, the character who was saying these inane things really believed in them.

* * *

Casey Nicholaw (now a director-choreographer) came to class with a longtime student of mine, Paige Price, when they were in "Saturday Night Fever" together. Casey continued in class for the next couple of years while going from show to show as an actor, until he transitioned to his new profession. Early on, he brought in his all-purpose up-tune one day and had us all laughing. The song is called "When I Grow Up (The G-Man Song)" by Harold Rome from "Pins and Needles," and the song itself is more charming than funny. Casey *made* it funny by performing it with the understated professionalism of an old-school second banana (vaudeville term: not the lead comic) and with choice bits of staging and business.

What was funny – the performer's easy touch and the staging.

* * *

Marilyn Caskey (now a voice and presentation coach in the business world) sang "You Could Drive a Person Crazy" from "Company" (Sondheim) as a solo. The song was written as a trio, in an Andrew Sisters style, with vocal fills between the lyric lines (sung on the syllable "doo"). In the trio version, the fills jump around from singer to singer, from low to high, to create a loony sense that these women are trying hard to not lose their grip. In her solo version, Marilyn sang all the parts herself, which made the struggle with losing her grip even harder. She appeared as if she had multiple personalities or was being visited by voices.

What was funny – the song is funny, but it's also famous, which can tend to diminish the comic effect of any song in a class or audition. But singing this famous trio as a solo is a funny idea, and here, the audience's knowledge of the song *added* to the comic effect.

Note: Marilyn used this song as a first audition for the role of Electra in the 2008 revival of "Gypsy" and got the role. Electra is one of the three strippers who sing "You Gotta Get A Gimmick." The women are older veterans of the trade, offering advice to newcomer Louise. In the show, Marilyn played her stripper with zero energy and enthusiasm. When she turned on the light switch in her costume, the costume twinkled but *she didn't*. Similar to her work in class, her performance was subtle, inventive, and very funny.

* * *

Marcus Stevens (also a gifted lyricist) sang "Mention My Name in Sheboygan" by Bob Hilliard, Dick Sanford, and Sammy Mysels. This is a clever 1947 novelty song in which the singer brags about his reputation in Sheboygan, Paducah, and Tacoma while also letting us know that whatever he did in those towns he left one step ahead of the police.

Similar to Casey's second banana in "The G-Man Song," Marcus' grifter had a vaudevillian dash to him, and similar to Lindsay's ultimate success with "Compromise," Marcus didn't play *down* to his character. This guy took pride in his exploits and his notoriety.

What was funny – the song and the zeal with which Marcus invited us to use his name to open doors.

* * *

Sutton Foster shocked us one day by singing a rousing solo version of "Oklahoma" (R&H). You know that "gusto" dancers have in big Golden Age dance numbers, where they're hooting and going "Yippee"? Well, Sutton had that gusto all by herself, while belting brilliantly. She apparently used to use this for chorus auditions, and it got results.

What was funny – nobody should sing "Oklahoma" as a solo, and she was completely invested in the manufactured gaiety we sometimes see in musicals.

* * *

Alisa Klein wrote a piece for herself called "This Is My 16 Bars." This was a terrifically clever audition piece for a dancer/singer who was constantly being asked for a 16-bar cut. In it, she sang very low and very high, and she got laughs and jobs with it.

What was funny – the ingenuity of the actor writing this piece for herself and the "know your audience" savvy of singing it for people who were spending their day listening to 16-bar cuts. But also, Alisa had an enthusiasm in performing it that was out of proportion to what was being said. I mean, why would someone be so enthusiastic about this? They wouldn't be. That's the funny part.

* * *

Kevin Covert (now the Director of the Musical Theater Program at Shenandoah University) had countless auditions for the original "Spamalot" and was determined to make his Broadway debut with this show. Kevin's book was overflowing with comic material, but 2 songs seemed especially right for the occasion, so we worked them again and again to make sure Kevin would feel confident and, hence, loose in his auditions.

"Poisoning Pigeons in the Park," by satirical 1950s songwriter Tom Lehrer, is fairly well known, so it was possible that the funny writing itself would not take Kevin's audience by surprise. But, in the song, Kevin was trying to tamp down his obvious delight so as not to appear crazy, which made him appear crazy. It seemed perfect for the show.

But his other choice was even better. "Who Played Poker with Pocahontas When John Smith Went Away?" was written in 1919 by Fred Albert, Sam Lewis, and Joe Young, and it was likely that no one would ever have heard it before. As Kevin sang the song, he was prudishly lit up about the possibility of impropriety and thrilled to be spreading the gossip further. He ended up using both songs and getting the job.

What was funny – the songs and the demented specificity of Kevin's approach to each of them.

* * *

This is an admittedly small sample, but even so, some patterns emerge. Everything that made us laugh was *focused*. The actors knew what they were doing in their scenes. Even in those cases where the actors were out-and-out "performing" as opposed to "acting" ("Oklahoma," "This Is My 16 Bars," and "The G-Man Song"), the energy and point of view of each performance was specific.

And in all the cases cited, the actors chose these pieces because they themselves thought they were funny. Very often, especially if you are shy about comedy, you might be guessing what's funny instead of choosing something that actually makes you yourself laugh.

I also see a pattern in the samples I cited where something potentially explosive in the character is being contained, with some difficulty. This aspect was present in "Fanny Pack," "You Could Drive a Person Crazy," "Poisoning Pigeons . . . ," and "Who Played Poker with Pocahontas . . . ." This sort of compression is a great tool for the actor. Harnessing an energy source like this allows you to use it to full advantage.

The most common mistake I see actors make with comic material (as with comedic shows) is that the energy of the performance is random and scattered. I spoke earlier about pretending to be "five happy people" and how exhausting it can be. That's what this fake, pumped-up energy is like. It blurts out, clanks off the walls, and falls to the floor.

I've often heard an actor say: "I want it to be fun," and I always think: "For whom?" It will be fun for the audience if you have a good piece of material, a good idea of how to approach it, and, most of all, if you don't try too hard. And it will be fun for you if you find the right comedic slant, stay focused, and have a good time.

* * *

Longtime student Annaleigh Ashford would often show all of us in class how to be fearless and focused in comedy. In an episode of the TV series "Smash," she played an actor doing a less than successful audition for the role of Marilyn Monroe in the show-within-the-show. She had brought "I Want to Be Loved by You" (Herbert Stothart, Bert Kalmar, and Harry Ruby) into class to prepare for her actual audition for the episode. Annaleigh had two possible approaches in mind: trying to be Marilyn Monroe or being a rank amateur, like the Parker Posey character in "Waiting for Guffman." She wanted to determine which approach was better, and in the process, I wanted to give

Annaleigh a workout by throwing her a number of adjustments in quick succession.

These are my notes from that session:

1 – trying to be Marilyn Monroe, doing the song as in "Some Like It Hot."
2 – someone like Parker Posey in "Waiting for Guffman."
3 – #2, with less parody, more real.
4 – #3 as a soprano, transposed up two steps.
5 – back to #3, original key.
6 – back to Marilyn, but this time let's say that you, the actor, also want to show your voice.
7 – more Marilyn, teasing, purring, lots of breath in the voice.
8 – combine #6 and 7. YES.
9 – Parker (just for us both to see it again).
10 – #8 again, define it even better, as if saying "these are my skills" and "I want the job." Also, lots of Marilyn.

Annaleigh chose #10, but from 1–10, her classmates and I were laughing and learning.

Seeing Annaleigh in "Kinky Boots," singing "The History of Wrong Guys" (a song we hadn't worked on together), I again saw this actor's great comic creativity combined with a laser-like focus. And what a fabulous combination, a character who is discombobulated and an actor who is focused.

In the years that followed, when young women would work on their auditions for this role in "Kinky Boots," they never knew whether to be Annaleigh or the character. Commendably, actors were encouraged by the associate director (D.B. Bonds) to make it their own, but after Annaleigh, that often proved impossible.

* * *

"I'm not funny" / "I can't sing rock"/ "I'm no good at traditional musical theater"/ "I hate this kind of song"/ "I don't sound contemporary."

I forgot to mention that these are all quotes from students. But if you're not funny, how come you make your friends laugh? If you can't sing rock, who was that at the karaoke bar? And if you're no good at traditional musical theater, what about when you sing the end of "Adelaide's Lament" in the shower? You can let yourself be good at everything!

Erika Henningsen and Barrett Wilbert Weed have become widely known for their superb performances in "Mean Girls." So, you might suppose that what they *do* is Contemporary Musical Theater. But, in their years in class, I saw each of them work out on, and excel at, every type of song we've talked about in this chapter, and *then* some.

Erika sang as many Golden Age songs and Standards in class as she did songs that were written in her lifetime. For her first class, she brought in the great Strouse and Adams song "I Want to Be With You," from "Golden Boy." And to hear her sing in her soprano register, you might easily assume that *that's* what she does.

I met Barrett when she was in "Bare" off-Broadway. In the five years we worked together, she had a natural affinity for the songs of Miller and Tysen, Kerrigan and Lowdermilk, Joe Iconis, and their contemporaries. But she was equally at home with Rodgers and Hart, Frank Loesser, Kander and Ebb, Joni Mitchell, John Mayer and Lin-Manuel Miranda.

Acting is acting, regardless of the type of material you are singing, and becoming proficient in as many different genres as possible will help you be brilliant in any one of them.

Once, in class, Erika was preparing to audition for a production of "Wonderful Town" (music by Leonard Bernstein, lyrics by Betty Comden and Adolf Green). She was given "Ohio" (a famous duet from the score) to sing for her audition. As part of her session, I wanted Erika to have a scene partner, so she could experience the physical and vocal togetherness the two homesick sisters have as they harmonize their way through this song. I asked if anyone in class knew the other part. Barrett did. Barrett (of "Bare" and "Heathers") knew the harmony part and all the words of this 1953 song.

These two may be known for their performances in "Mean Girls," but you should see them do "Ohio."

6

INVISIBLE PARTNERS

Let's say you are singing to another person in the scene, something that has come up in many of the songs we've talked about so far.

In an audition, the person we see is you. Through your behavior in the scene/song, you are telling us that there is *another* person in the room, and by where you choose to focus, you are telling us where that invisible partner is. The focal point is usually somewhere behind the people you're auditioning for, most often to the center of the wall behind them, or slightly to either side of center. There is a time-honored tradition of singing to a spot on the wall in auditions. Having a stationary focal point is indeed the simplest and usually the best choice to make. But early in my teaching experience, I began exploring how to use this device well, and when the focal point is meant to be an invisible partner, this is what I've found . . .

In life, you've had many experiences where you've told a story to someone, or confided in them, or confronted, implored, bargained with, or opened up to another person. When you do this, you will notice that your gaze does not stay constantly fixed on them. At times, you look away to gather your thoughts, to collect the imagery or words you then bring to them. Or you might look away because saying this directly to them feels too intense, or because you are choosing to be indirect in the scene, or simply because we don't tend to stare at the people we're talking to.

But as actors, we *do* sometimes stare at a spot on the wall, when we're trying to prove to the people watching that the spot is another person. This is a false behavior, and it can cause the actor to appear rigid or absent.

It is an equally false behavior to try to artificially create the effect of "collecting your thoughts" or "employing an indirect tactic" by deliberately looking away from time to time. Once again, true behavior is true, and false is false. But you have a world of experience with this true behavior in life. We don't even realize we're doing it, but we are. And similarly, in your acting, it becomes second nature when you're actually engaged in something more important, the action of your song.

You don't have to prove to us that the focal point is a person, by either staring at it or by simulating the realistic behavior of *not* staring at it. *The spot on the wall is simply where you've decided to place your partner.* Any additional impression we get or evidence we see of that other person will be in *you*. This will occur naturally through your behavior and in the colors we see as you take action in your scene.

To practice this technique, choose a song you would sing to another person. Find a real scene partner to rehearse with and, of course, know who that scene partner is meant to represent and why you are singing to them. Now, start your work-out on the song by positioning the other person fairly close to you, say three or four feet away, face to face. Assuming this has been successful, the next time through the song, place the live partner at a greater distance, against the wall, where the "spot" would be. Then, remove the partner, but keep the spot. This is what we are meaning to do when the spot on the wall is representing an invisible partner. If you feel yourself slipping into unnatural behaviors without the partner, bring them back. Then, remove them again.

* * *

Here's a completely different way of approaching the act of singing to someone who isn't there. Again, know who you're singing to and why, and again choose a spot, simply because having a relatively stationary focal point is more attractive and less distracting than the alternative. In this approach, however, we will not use a live scene partner during the work-out. Instead, consider only what is true at this moment. You are in this room you're in, and the person you're singing to is actually wherever they are, whether that is ten blocks away or in Australia. If you don't know where they are, where would you think they are? Imagine it, picture it. That's where they are. Now sing to them.

I came up with this technique when looking to have even less make-believe in the act of singing to an invisible partner.

Try it. I think you'll be surprised how easy it is and how different it is from the first technique.

In this approach, you are still more or less using the spot on the wall, but now the invisible partner is in *you*, in your thoughts and your feelings. Perhaps you are rehearsing what you will say to them, or reliving what you *did* say, or even better, what you *didn't* say. Or maybe you are summoning them, or trying to dispel them.

Summoning? Dispelling? That would suggest that I think you have powers. I do. Don't you sometimes know when your phone is going to ring, or haven't you ever thought of someone you've not seen or thought of in years, and hours later, you bump into them on the street? You have powers.

* * *

Here's another technique. Going back to working with a live scene partner, I've found some ways to give the actor the experience of the partner being both real and invisible. These exercises once again remove a layer of make-believe from the act of singing to a person who isn't there. As before, know who the scene partner represents and why you're singing to that person. This time, though, *begin* with your partner against the wall, where your focal point will be. After that, put them in the next room; literally, put the scene partner in the next room, on the other side of the wall. You can't see them, but you know they're there. In this exercise, don't try to reach them with additional volume. But *do* try to reach them.

Or how about this? Place the scene partner behind you, at a distance of at least six feet, and, as always, sing to a spot in front of you. Wonderfully simple, isn't it?

I first did this in class with Elizabeth Stanley, when she was playing Elvis Presley's girlfriend in "Million Dollar Quartet," because her song "Fever" (by Eddie Cooley and Otis Blackwell) was staged this way in the show. Elizabeth was singing the song downstage at a microphone, facing the audience. Elvis was hanging out upstage, listening as she sang. Without making any physical reference to his being behind her, she felt his presence and was singing to him. Working in class with both Elizabeth and her replacement in "Million Dollar Quartet," Victoria Matlock, I came to see the value of this positioning of the two people as yet another way to approach singing to an invisible partner.

In both of these configurations, with the partner in the next room or placed behind you, the other person could actually leave, and you might not even know it. You would think they were still there. But that's the whole game, isn't it? You believe the partner is there, so they are.

* * *

What if the song you're singing refers to the physical proximity of another person, or to touching or holding them as you sing? "Is It Really Me?" (by Jones and Schmidt) does this in such lines as: "Now here I am, safe in your arms." In Rodgers and Hammerstein's "Younger Than Springtime," you sing "My eyes look down at your lovely face" and other lines that seem to specify a certain physicality.

If you were in a production of "110 In the Shade" or "South Pacific," the other character would be present. But if you were *auditioning* for one of these shows, or using one of these songs for an unrelated audition or concert, you would most likely be working with an invisible partner.

In these situations, you do not need to show us the physicality you refer to in the lyric. You do not need to show us the embrace. Ultimately, we only need to see the *effect* the embrace has on you. And this comes from *inside* you.

Once again, you will probably be singing to a stationary focal point. Here are two exercises you can do with a live scene partner that can help you arrive at the state of "closeness" being spoken of in these songs.

In the first, stand next to each other, approximately five feet apart, with both of you facing forward. Each of you should raise the arm nearest the partner until your fingertips touch. Increase or decrease the distance between you until only the tips of your fingers are touching. Remain facing forward throughout the song.

In the second, face forward, this time with your partner a foot or so behind you, also facing forward. Just before you begin to sing, your scene partner should gently place an open hand between your shoulder blades, in back of where your heart is, and leave it there throughout the song.

These exercises are intended to sensitize you to closeness, to touch, to the presence of the partner, so when the partner is no longer there, the sensations are easier to call upon.

It's possible in these types of situations that when you transition to working solely with the invisible partner, you will be tempted to place that partner right in front of you, say a foot or two away from you, as opposed to the greater distance against the wall. This is an understandable instinct, given the physicality referred to in the lyric and the intimacy you may have just experienced in the exercises. But this positioning of the invisible partner is not practical. First of all, when you place the other person close to you with no wall behind them, you cannot help but use an abundance of energy trying to *see* them there, as if you were attempting to call up a hologram. But also, this imagined closeness can cause you to sing softly, in an effort to recapture the intimacy of the exercise.

But the intimacy is not about the size of the sound; it's about the intensity of the connection. This and *all* the positive effects of your performance will come from inside you. You are what we see and hear. You are what is portable. The other person is not in the room.

Often in class, when a student has had a particularly good session with a live scene partner, they will ask jokingly: "Can I bring them with me to the audition?" The answer is "yes." It takes practice, but of course you can.

7

AUDITIONING

Obviously, there are entire books and courses devoted to this subject, but I believe the act of auditioning relies less on rules and more on instinct than others might think. Yes, there are specific steps to be taken: entering the room, engaging with the people behind the table (if they initiate the action), communicating with the accompanist, walking from the piano to the center of the room, taking a breath, a moment to prepare, nodding to the accompanist, and singing. And we will deal with these nuts and bolts.

But most of what I have to say on the subject of auditioning is about how to be truly present in the room and how to maintain your ability to act in the face of all the external distractions that come your way at auditions.

I spoke in the preface of this book about "trusting your instincts rather than guessing what other people want you to be." This is never truer than it is in the audition room. The wish to please, or in this case the wish to get the job, can cause actors to abandon their technique and experience and simply aim at the qualities they think the people in the room want to see.

But understand this: if there are multiple people behind the table, there is no consensus about what they're looking for. They may think there is, but having been in many of these groups, I can tell you, there isn't. Casting is totally subjective. It's an imperfect, at times random, process. So, your best chance of getting hired is in being prepared, present, and truly alive.

You arrive at the audition.
The monitor says: "You're next."
The actor before you exits the audition room.
The monitor ushers you in and says your name to the team.
Someone at the table says: "Hello."
You go to the piano, put your music up, and give a tempo.
You walk out to the center of the room, nod to the accompanist and go.
You sing decently but feel detached in your acting.

Rewind. Same day, different scenario.
You hear from your agent that morning that you just booked a good job.
    It conflicts with the one you're supposed to audition for today.
The agent advises you to go to the audition anyway.
You get to the audition fifteen minutes early.
When checking in, you glance at the list and notice the number of people there are before you.
You go to the bathroom, and while washing your hands you say to yourself in the mirror: "You got a job."
You sit back in the hallway, close your eyes, and think about the song you're going to sing.
Eyes open now, you wish "good luck" to the person before you.
The monitor says: "You're next."
The actor before you exits the audition room.
The monitor ushers you in and says your name to the team.
Someone at the table says: "Hello."
You look at them and say "hello" back.

Two other people who had been talking to each other look up.
One of them says: "Hi."
You smile.
You go to the piano, regard the accompanist as a human being, put your music up on the piano, and point out something in the arrangement that might be tricky.
You take a breath, give a tempo, and walk out to the center of the room.
You take a moment and a breath, and allow yourself to be filled with everything you need to act the song beautifully.
Then, you nod to the accompanist and go.
The performance goes well.

Of course, it's easy for me to invent two opposing scenarios in order to make my point. But the only real invention here was in my turning back the clock on the actor's day to play the scene twice. In reality, every actor I know has had these two auditions.

To Analyze the Differences

Before the second audition, while you were still at home, something good happened, something that then went with you to the audition and colored everything you did.

I wonder, is there a way to create that feeling without having received the good news? And if not, is there a way to at least have the improved sense of presence and communication you had in the second audition without any help from the fates?

Be on time. Be early. This is in your control. I'm sure you've heard of self-sabotage. Well, being late is a shining example of it.
Whether at the bathroom mirror or just in your thoughts, be kind to yourself. Stop silently speaking ill of yourself. How do I know you do this? Because I do it, and because I've known thousands of actors.
If you're in the waiting room and you want to be alone so you can center yourself and prepare, close your eyes. Breathe slowly and deeply. Think about the work you want to do in the audition; not the impression you want to make, but the work you want to do.

Be generous to the other auditioners. When the monitor ushers you into the room and says your name, be yourself and be present. If someone at the table initiates a conversation or says a simple "hello," be responsive. If they don't, that's fine too.

When you go to the piano, treat the accompanist with respect. Give any information you need to give cleanly and clearly. Take a breath, and hear the tempo in your head before you give it.

Walk out to the center of the room, as yourself, not in the character of the song, and not as a non-person. You're in the center of the room now. Take a moment and a breath and allow yourself to be filled with everything you need in order to act the song beautifully. Then, nod to the accompanist and go.

If your song has a piano intro of any length, as opposed to a bell-tone, you may find that you're able to prepare *during* that intro, instead of before it. Either way, take the breath before you nod.

Note: You may have been taught that upon reaching the center of the room you should state your name and the title of your song. And it's quite possible that there are some academic settings and Unified Auditions in which this is a useful tool. But in a professional setting, this formality is no longer common practice. As a rule, the casting director has already put your resume in front of the team, and your name is the next one on our audition sheets. As for your song's title, it will reveal itself as you sing. If we don't happen to know the song, and are interested, it's possible that the question would cause an exchange between you and the team after you sing, which would not be a bad thing at all.

* * *

What *You* Do/What *They* Do

Choose a song for the audition and coach it with someone you trust. Plan on bringing three or four other pieces to the audition that you think could be useful, and be prepared to sing them. Don't carry songs with you to the audition that you wouldn't want to sing.

If they ask you to sing something other than the song you've planned on, relax and go with it. This could end up being the best audition you will ever have. If you've been asked to learn a piece from the show, learn it well. Coach it with someone you trust. Type a lyric sheet and, if you need it, *use it*. A lyric sheet also reminds us that this is an audition and not opening night.

Do not concern yourself with the behavior of those behind the table while you are singing. I, for instance, don't look at a resume until the actor has sung a bit, because I don't want to be unduly influenced by the actor's good credits or lack of them. Then, I'll look at the resume as the actor continues. In other words, some of us may be looking down at the table during some of your audition.

You may also see or hear us talking to each other. In my experience, this is almost always a good thing. Someone is probably saying to someone else: "I like this actor, do you?"

If you are asked to do a song or scene a second time with an adjustment, listen, relax, and take the direction. You don't have to be perfect, and you don't have to set aside your skills to achieve what's being asked for. Ideally, your skills will *help* you take the direction.

Occasionally, after you sing or read, the people you're auditioning for may be unsure what they want to do. This is not a bad thing. Just *be* there, until they make the next move.

Actors are sometimes uncomfortable when there is "air" in an audition. For example, earlier in this chapter, one of the big differences between the first and second versions of the audition was that the first audition had no air in it. But in the second one, you let the audition breathe. There was "air" when you acknowledged the "hello" as you entered, when you took a bit more time with the accompanist, and when you gave yourself a breath before nodding to begin. Cumulatively, this probably amounted to no more than seven or eight seconds, but it made a world of difference. And *this* moment (where they're deciding how to proceed) also has air in it. Just let it be there.

When deciding what to wear to an audition, I think it's best to dress as yourself, with a subtle eye toward the world of the show. "Dressing up" can make it look as though you're wearing a costume, and "dressing down" can be seen as disrespect for the project, unless, of course, dressing down is right for the show.

Should you wear the same thing to the callback? Yes, definitely. If there are multiple callbacks, should you still wear the same thing? If you wish to, adapt it, vary it, but keep it close.

What about hair? I would suggest you not change your hairstyle for a callback, unless you've been asked to. We've called you back because we're interested. A completely different hairstyle may make you look like a different person.

* * *

When the Spot on the Wall is Not an Invisible Partner

Sometimes you're singing to the universe or to yourself. In Chapter 1, we talked about these choices and what each might mean, but we didn't talk about where to focus in these cases.

As described in Chapter 1, when you're singing to yourself, it's as if there are two of you or two halves of you. I find this imagery useful because it points the performance outward instead of inward. And in terms of "where to focus," it allows "singing to yourself" to be handled just as you might handle other invisible partners.

Singing to the universe is another matter. While I still think having a relatively stationary focal point is best, how you play to that spot may vary depending on how you define the universe. If your universe is, for instance, the ocean, that might affect how you use the spot on the wall.

As for the heavens or God, looking up is not a workable option, just as looking down would not be a workable option if you were singing to the Grand Canyon. For these reasons, the traditional spot on the wall seems to be traditional for good reason.

Stories, however, want to have an audience, so unless you are telling your story to a single invisible partner, you are probably singing to a group, real or imagined.

You can sing directly above the people you're auditioning for and use your lower peripheral vision as a guide, to achieve the effect of telling your story to them, without actually looking them in the eye.

If you want to sing to an invisible group that is populated by a specific category of people, like high school freshmen, or all your aunts and uncles, I find the image of a grandstand or hillside to be extremely useful. Putting your invisible group on such a slope allows you to move your focus around to address them all in a believable fashion.

When working with a student on "It's Hard to Speak My Heart" from "Parade" (Jason Robert Brown), I might begin by having the actor sing to his classmates, with the group being noticeably unmoved by his plea. Then working without those live partners, the actor can easily populate the hillside or grandstand with just such a group.

Briana Carlson-Goodman would sing "Cornet Man" from "Funny Girl" (Jule Styne and Bob Merrill) to the front row of a balcony full of women. This choice suited the song because her specific audience was likely to be both fired up and fully supportive of her complaint about men. Also, though, by placing herself in a theater, she allowed the song to be a performance on a stage, a quality this song has in its very fiber.

When Briana first brought this song into class in 2010, she was in "Hair" at The Al Hirschfeld Theatre. The Hirschfeld has a balcony that hangs very low over the orchestra level, so it feels close to you when you're on that stage. This, of course, was the balcony she used. So, not only was the audience specific, so was the balcony.

Singing to the Reader

This can be useful for callbacks when you're singing from the show you're auditioning for, assuming it suits the material. You may recall that in Chapter 1, Brandon Uranowitz prepared to use this technique in his "Falsettos" callback. It's an especially attractive option when you've already been engaged in doing book scenes with the reader. One drawback is that it can cause you to face downward, but you can minimize this effect by making sure you have a bit of distance from the reader.

16-Bar Auditions

Doing 16-bar cuts (and at times, as little as 8 bars) can be frustrating for the actor. You do so much prep and you wait sometimes for hours for the opportunity to sing for half a minute. But I can tell you from having been at these audition days that those of us behind the table become accustomed to this shorter length and can actually see and hear a great deal from such an audition.

You can find great cuts, ones that feature your singing and also allow us to experience your acting. To find them, bring five of your best audition songs to a talented music helper. You will find at least one good cut, probably two.

In life, we sometimes say things of great import that only take a few seconds, shorter than 8 bars. And remember our discussion about "Changing My Major," how it is valuable to not know how long your song is? This point can be applied equally to songs that last six minutes and fragments that last fifteen seconds. What are you "doing?" What are you saying? And why have you broken the silence to say it? These are the things that matter.

I have a new show in the works called "Poster Boy" (with book writer Joe Tracz), and one of the most effective musical moments in it is only a minute and twenty seconds long. A character named Harrison blurts out what he has to say and leaves the stage. We do that in life. We can do it in our songs.

Your 16-bar cut may come out slugging, or it may rev up in the first few measures. Look at "Some People" in "Gypsy" (Styne and Sondheim). It starts full-throttle and never lets up. Your cut can work like that, if it's smartly chosen and well-acted.

Feedback

You are sometimes given feedback to incorporate into your callback. This can be useful, but being *overly* responsive to it may cause you to leave behind the other values that got you called back in the first place. No one intends for you to do this.

As for feedback after the fact (a reason given for you not being chosen), very often you will not receive any. When informing your agent that you didn't get the job, the casting agent will likely say something general like: "We went another way." This is a kindness, a shorthand that allows the casting director to deliver the information quickly and professionally without saying something negative about you to justify their actions.

Your frustration and confusion may cause you to push for more information. It's best not to do this. Anything further you hear in this delicate situation will stay with you like the ghost of an old tattoo you've tried to have removed. Besides, most often, you aren't really asking for guidance or advice when you do this. You're saying: "You were wrong not to hire me. Why did you do such a stupid thing?"

For all you know, you are next in line for the role. Or the composer loved you and will remember you. Or the reader is directing a play next month and wants to see you for the lead. Leave it alone. You'll be glad you did.

Final thought: You don't have to do anything to make us like you. Be genuine. Be present. That's what you can do. You don't have to be "nice." Nor do you have to hide your power to win favor. Just show up, be alert, alive, able to listen, ready for anything, and eager to play.

8

A SENSE OF PLAY

In 1980, while working on "Is There Life After High School?" with book writer Jeffrey Kindley, I saw his preschool-aged son playing on the floor with a miniature wooden barnyard filled with three-dimensional wooden animals. He was positioning the livestock around the barnyard in a very specific way that only he knew the purpose of. Among the animals were three horses and two cows. He said aloud to himself: "I need another cow." So, he picked up one of the horses and spoke to it: "You're a cow now." And that was that. The horse became a cow.

In the summer of 1956, I saw the film of "Moby Dick" at the age of seven with my brother, James, and a pair of twin boys from our neighborhood. After the movie, the four of us bought a huge bag of cheap balloons at the stationery store, went back to the twins' house, and, with the help of a garden hose, had a raucous water balloon fight.

This comes to mind because, during the fight, I was not one of four skinny boys in a suburban backyard. I was a grown man, fighting for my life, on the high seas. And I wasn't acting, I was playing.

As we get into the double-digit ages of eleven, twelve, and thirteen, most of us lose the ability to play. In fact, we run from it, scorn it, try to stomp it out in our frenzy to become grown-ups. And yet, the ability to play is an essential tool for the actor.

In 2016, my daughter Daisy was cast in an immersive musical, "The Bad Years" (Book and Lyrics by Kate Kerrigan, Music by Brian Lowdermilk, Direction by Stephen Brackett). Staged in a Brooklyn warehouse, the set was laid out to be the interior of a ranch house. The characters (all "twenty-something") were attending a party in that house, and the audience was free to roam through the structure however they wished. There were always multiple scenes going on, and often two or three songs being sung in different rooms, at the same time.

Daisy went into the process having no idea what it would feel like to be in something so free-wheeling and unpredictable. Truly, no two performances would ever be alike.

As it turned out, having to be light on her feet and ready to play at every performance ended up teaching her as much about acting as I ever have.

In Chapter 5 ("Types of Songs"), how did Lindsay Northen so easily *become* her castmate for the Heisler and Goldrich song "Compromise?" Doing the song as that other person caused it to ring true, and hence be funny. But how did she *do* that? What combination of insights and skills allowed her to make this seemingly effortless transformation?

Part of the answer came from Lindsay's day-to-day experience with this woman. She knew her and knew her well; her thought processes, her cadences, and her propensity for giving unsolicited advice and too much information.

Another part goes back to our discussion of what a character knows and what they don't know. Looked at this way, the character isn't a fool; there are simply some things she doesn't know. And, to paraphrase a line from earlier, "to not know those things is to be the character."

But the final piece of the puzzle is "play." Just as the preschooler turned that horse into a cow, Lindsay turned herself into this other woman. She just *did* it. We are always asking our audience for a "suspension of disbelief." As actors, we are often asking it of ourselves too.

* * *

Sometimes, the character we need to inhabit in a song is someone we ourselves might have been, had our lives unfolded differently, had we chosen to move to the city, or stay in our hometown, or live in a foreign country, or have a family in our 20s, or pursue a different career, or follow a love to Tahiti, or perform motorcycle stunts and end up losing the use of our right hand. All of these occurrences would have altered our development, and that other person, that person we aren't, can be accessible to us in our acting.

I raised a very big question in an earlier chapter. "What do you do if you've never experienced anything like what you're being asked to inhabit?" I gave one possible answer to the question when discussing empathy. This idea of an "alternate life" is another.

There's a famous song by John Prine called "Angel from Montgomery" in which a woman sings passionately about her wish to be spirited away from her dead marriage and featureless existence.

I've worked on this song with a number of students and at times approached it as an alternate life, one the actor might have lived had she made different choices early in her life.

The "person you might have become" is, again, someone you know very well. As you were choosing which crossroad to take, you saw this other person and, in this case, you feared what you saw.

As always with good writing, the song will do much of the work for you, but your sense of play, however dark the game may be, will enable you to *become* this other person.

I've seen this "alternate life" technique work magically for my students. Emily Afton used it to great effect in the song "Pearl's a Singer" (Leiber, Stoller, Dino, & Sembello) to book the role of Pattie in a production of "Smokey Joe's Café," and Jennifer Bowles (who understudied Miss

Honey in "Matilda" on Broadway before taking over the role on the road) used it in her beautiful work on *this* delicious character.

* * *

I will occasionally ask a student to sing a song as their mother or father. This is surprisingly easy to do and can have a profound effect on your performance.

In life, you have probably spent a fair amount of time trying to *be* your parents and at least as much time trying *not* to be them. The peculiar thing about this is that, for the actor, these two extremes are not opposites; they're second cousins, and either one of them can prove useful when trying to step into your parents' shoes.

My father's shoes came to him free of charge, from the Veteran's Administration. He wore one, identical style of shoe throughout his entire post-war life: sturdy, dark brown Oxfords. The left shoe had a leg brace built into the heel that then extended 10 or 12 inches up the leg, with a flat metal shaft on each side and a thick leather collar at the top. I would often clomp around in those shoes, leg brace and all, and would sometimes wear one of his fedoras while doing it.

What was I doing if not trying to be him? Yet, I've spent most of my adult life trying to *not* be him. He hated his job as an accountant. I love my work as a writer and a teacher, and I chose these professions so I could be my own boss and spend each day being inventive, thereby ensuring that I would *not* be him.

But he was a perfectionist, with a work ethic to match, as am I. And his chemistry had a strong downward pull to it, as does mine. But I fight back against the pull, which was never in his nature to do.

There's a song I wrote for "Working" called "Joe." It's a character study of a retired man, lower middle class, blue collar or very modest white collar. The language of the song has a Brooklynese lilt to it, to fit the cheerful shrug with which the character gives us an account of his daily activities. Studs Terkel's great book, "Working," was most certainly my main source for the song. But I also used my father. When writing the song at the age of 28, I let myself be him. And when performing it, which I've done often over the years, I once again step into those VA Oxfords.

Singing a song as one of your parents can also yield astounding results when you imagine that *you* are the person they're singing to. It can be you now or you at any age you choose.

Look, for instance, at the song "Anyone Can Whistle," spoken about in Chapter 1. Imagine singing that lyric as one of your parents and the person being sung to is you. Quite something, isn't it?

* * *

Today, though you may have never thought about it, there are different ages you feel. Take a moment with that idea, if you would. What are your ages? They're all true, and they're all yours. Your list may include an age greater than your own. It is not uncommon, for instance, for a college student to feel 5, 18, and 30.

You can easily play yourself at any of those ages, or you can be yourself now, but bring *all* the ages you feel with you. At our most genuine, I believe this is what we're already doing, and as an actor you can tap into this natural complexity at any moment, by simply allowing yourself to be all your various ages at once.

Here at my desk this evening, I know myself to be 11, 19, 41, 51, and 70, and every one of them is having a hand in writing this chapter.

* * *

At times in my adult life, when I wish to appear more reasonable than I am, I'll find myself imitating my brother, his considerate manner and calm voice. I've mentioned this to him, and he tells me that, to some degree, *he's* acting too. Which suggests what?

One, that just as it is easy to "play" one of your parents, it may be easy to play a sibling. After all, these are the people we probably spent the most time with in our first fifteen or sixteen years.

But, also, it suggests that there are occasions when we may be "acting the role of ourselves." The great novelist John Updike once wrote: "Life, just as we first thought, is playing grown-up." *Playing.*

* * *

Was there a dress-up basket among your playthings, or perhaps just a favorite prop or piece of grown-up clothing you played with, a top-hat and cane, your mother's high heels? Did you put on shows in your garage, your basement, your room, your head?

In Chapter 3, I introduced you to Betsy Morgan, who had been Kelli O'Hara's standby in "The King and I." In Chapter 1, you met Alex Finke, who played Johanna in The Barrow Street Theater production of "Sweeney Todd."

Well, Betsy was also in that Barrow Street production, playing two roles, the Beggar Woman and Pirelli. For her callbacks, we worked on the Beggar Woman's section of "No Place Like London," and Pirelli's solo, "The Contest." For the first piece, we concentrated on combining the life and death stakes of the character with Betsy's first-rate singing.

For the second, however, we used "play." The character is a conceited fop of a barber with a fake Italian accent and a comic expansiveness not usually seen in serious musical theater. And the fact that a woman was being cast to play the role only added to the cartoonish portrait of male self-adoration that is Pirelli.

As Betsy worked on the song, it reminded me of the abandon children have when playing dress-up. You pull out a tutu, a pair of red suspenders, or a cape, and presto, you're someone else. That's what Betsy was doing; she was playing, showing off, having fun.

Six months into the run, seven months pregnant, Betsy left the show. By then her Pirelli costume had been altered to accommodate her changing shape, a character trait they decided to retain for Betsy's replacement.

Stacie Bono, a classmate of Betsy's, had multiple auditions for that job. She had been in class for about a year at that point with great results, but these sessions were particularly fascinating. Instead of trying to copy her classmate's performance of these songs, she was trying to make use of the tools that had led to such good results in the first place. For instance, the operatic size of the Beggar Woman's plea was made as much by the character's desperation as it was the vocal prowess of the singer.

This point keeps coming back in the book because it keeps coming back in every actor's experience. You have years of vocal training, then you spend additional time with the specific vocal demands of any given piece, but then, having done all of that, you use the voice to *express* feeling, not represent or replicate it.

As for Pirelli, this was the harder of the two tasks for Stacie. She had seen how ridiculous Betsy had allowed herself to be as the character. But the sense of play this moment called for was more difficult for her to access. My notes from early in her first Pirelli session included such unhelpful phrases from the teacher as "Don't be shy" and "Go further." Then, something useful: "Holding back is what feels foolish, committing to the game will allow you to fully play it."

Cut to the next scene. Stacie is downtown playing these great roles, and her Pirelli has the same pronounced potbelly that had been devised to accommodate her classmate's pregnancy.

* * *

On the first page of this chapter, I spoke of losing the ability to play as we get into our preteens and teens. Well, to contradict that notion, if we pursue acting in plays and musicals in those years, we may very well retain some part of this gift.

There is a raw chutzpah and a childish know-how that bounds onto the stage with us in a high school show. Then, as we become professionals, we again have a tendency to disown this showy behavior. But we still *need* it.

Look at Bert Lahr singing "If I Were King of the Forest" in "The Wizard of Oz." He's using a 6-year-old's dress-up basket, a 15-year-old's blind courage, and a consummate professional's craft and experience to make that performance. He's playing!

Sometimes, when a student is singing an old-style, razz-ma-tazz song like one I referenced earlier, "Cornet Man," we will work on acting first. In that song, there's the act of telling the story and the task of finding the truth in the character's complaint. But then, after that, I have been known to say: "Now, do what you would have done when you were 15."

I don't know if I was any good in the musicals I did at that age. But I can say that the boldest steps I ever took in high school were taken on that stage, in one production or another.

9

IN PRODUCTION

I saw a play on Broadway some decades ago that began with the main character addressing the audience in a serious monologue. During this, a latecomer came down the aisle and clumsily made their way to a seat in the center of the third or fourth row of the orchestra. The actor continued for about ten seconds of this and then stopped. The stop was stunning. He went from doing something detached and devoid of feeling to something scary and very present.

He then lectured the latecomer, saying something or other about lateness, after which he took a beat to compose himself. Looking up at the ceiling of the theater, he quickly recited to himself the last four or five lines he had spoken to find his place.

Then, he looked at the audience once again and clicked back into his planned performance. And I thought: "This is what he's going to be doing for the next two and a half hours: a tired recitation, a programmed sequence of line readings."

I've been in a number of audiences where an actor has paused to scold someone for their cellphone going off. I've seen performances stopped for collapsing sets, city-wide blackouts, and heart attacks in the audience.

But in the incident at the top of the page, an actor who was supposedly speaking to the audience stopped to speak to the audience, and then returned to speaking to the audience, with the unscripted portion being the only one that had any juice to it.

To be clear, I don't think breaking the fourth wall to lecture the audience about their behavior is ever a good idea. But in the case cited, the stylistic use of direct address in the play had already told the audience that there *was* no fourth wall. The actor's tangle with the latecomer proved this to be a lie.

People love seeing animals onstage, and it's not just because they're cute. It's because they might do *anything*. This absence of predictability is riveting. You can have this too. While saying and singing everything you're supposed to say and sing, and while being in the right place at every moment, you can be fully alive onstage.

This brings me to Brian d'Arcy James, pictured on the cover of this book, singing "At the Fountain," in "Sweet Smell of Success." Brian was never my student, but his work epitomizes everything I teach.

He played Sidney Falco in the show, a hungry press agent in the dirty, glamorous world of New York nightlife in 1952. The great John Lithgow played JJ Hunsecker, a ruthless, all-powerful columnist (winning a Tony Award for his performance), and Kelli O'Hara dazzled in her first major Broadway role as JJ's much younger half-sister, Susan.

In the story, JJ has just this night taken Sidney under his wing and given him a clutch of new clients, a quick trip to the tailor, and a name change (from Falcone to Falco). During all of this, the ensemble sings "Welcome to the Night" (music by Marvin Hamlisch, lyrics by Craig Carnelia). In the song, they simultaneously welcome and warn Sidney with such lines as:

We heard a rumor you were sniffin' at the bait
Flirtin' with your fate tonight

You got an angel and he's pickin' up the tab
Grab what you can grab tonight

Help yourself to a freebee
JJ's bein' nice
Oh, but what will the fee be?
Freebees have a price

Sidney is in disbelief, or rather, he has scraped and scrounged for so long that he chooses to revel in the welcome and overlook the warning – in "At the Fountain" (by Hamlisch and Carnelia):

You put the old suit in the trash
You take the whole damn past and cash it in
Cash the whole thing in
You're not crazy

A lot can happen in one night
With half a chance who knows what might begin
Falcone might just win

So many times you thought the way was clear
Only to find you can't get there from here

Here's your chance
Make some dough
Change your name
Keep the 'O'

Hey Sidney, you finally found some luck
You've always been an also-ran
Just racing for a buck
A guy with a smile
A way with a word
Quick with a joke
We've already heard

Y'ever hear the one about Lana Turner? Sittin' at the soda fountain, dreamin' her soda fountain dreams?

But there was something he could see
For just a moment
It's like he saw inside of me
What's really there
What I was
What I am
What I'll be

Maybe I'm at the fountain
Maybe I'm at the start
It's time to step up and drink
And not even think
You don't have to think to be smart

Sometimes the perfect timing
Feels like a work of art
'Cause it can bring you your break
And answer the ache
He offers, you take the part
Garbo Brando Harlow Monroe
Keep the 'O'
Garbo Brando Harlow Monroe
Keep the 'O'

Somebody buys a paper at the stand
Buddy, you hold my future in your hand

Fortunes change
People grow
Now and then
Fountains flow

It's like he saw inside of me
Where I belong, what I could be
And in the flashing of the neon
I could swear that he could see
What's really there

Garbo Brando Harlow Falco!

Looks like I'm at the fountain
Looks like I'm at the start
Before a door can be shut
You go with your gut
Yes, go with your gut and your heart

It's time to tear through that door
It's time now to soar
So, let my life story start

One day in rehearsal, just before we went out of town with the show, I saw Brian "find his performance" in this song. It was late in the day, with only a few of us still in the room: the director Nicholas Hytner, production supervisor Peter von Mayrhauser, associate conductor Ron Melrose, Brian, and me.

He had sung this song many times before, and it had been (I thought) everything we could ask for. But this day, he did something even better, something that, in hindsight, embodied so much of what we've been talking about in this book.

- His character had never said these things before. So, the actor *became* the author, thereby becoming the character.
- He felt his way through the song, line by line, section by section, just as we've been discussing.
- He was singing to himself and the universe, and for Sidney Falcone, the universe was New York City. Looking at this book's cover photo (with Bob Crowley's set and Natasha Katz' lighting), the city seems to be embracing Sidney while he reaches wide to embrace it back.
- The exultation he was expressing was alloyed with other elements, such as relief, and a hunger that had finally been assuaged, and (something I wouldn't have expected in this character) a kind of innocence.

- And, being the actor he is, I then saw Brian have the craft to be able to do this many times over.

* * *

Every musical and every director are different. So, you might think it would be difficult to apply the lessons of this book to the wide variety of situations you'll encounter. But these basic principles and techniques are flexible enough to be carried into any room. And you can use them at every step of the production process.

Half of the work you do during rehearsal is done with other people: the director, musical director, choreographer, and fellow actors. But half of your work is done by you alone. This back and forth between your public and private work allows the two to constantly inform each other.

On the first day of rehearsal, the director will usually articulate their vision for the piece and their expectations of you. All you need to do is listen.

Then, you will most likely be learning music for the first couple of days.

When the vocal parts are being taught by the musical director, *record them*, and as you sing in these learning sessions, *sing with energy*. Even if you are a quick learner, repetition is still of great use. It's an opportunity to start getting the music in your body, not just your head. Also, it is important for the musical director (and on a new show, the composer) to be able to assess the vocal parts and balance them.

If you need additional work to learn the music, other than your time in rehearsal, it is your responsibility to put in that extra time on your own. If you find the melody difficult or a particular rhythm tricky, try to figure out why it does what it does, the way we did earlier with "Millwork" and "My Heart Is So Full of You." If you can *understand* it, rather than just trying to memorize it, you will surely be able to learn it. This will also give you an ownership of what you've learned that will enable you to sing and act it even better. If you really do need more time on something, ask the musical director, and you will most likely be given what you need.

After the music is learned, customarily there will be a rough read/sing-through at a table, so the creative team and cast can have their first live experience of the piece. You do not need to turn in a polished performance at this read-through, not at all. But you do need to engage, listen, respond, and sing with purpose. This may be the last chance anyone (including you) gets to hear the whole show for the next week or so.

The steps that follow vary from show to show. There may be several days where the characters, the script, and the songs are explored as you all work through the play around a table. Just as commonly, though, the director and choreographer may begin staging the show from the top.

Whether you begin with table-work or staging, your "private" rehearsal work will take every bit of attention you're willing to give it. Let's say, for instance, you've just been given a piece of blocking: enter up right and cross to down left. You make the move, so that now you're standing down left while the director deals with getting three other actors onto the stage. During this time (let's call it two minutes), you could stand and wait for the sequence of four entrances to be run again, or you could be working by yourself. "Why does my character enter when they do?" "Where am I coming from?" "Why do I stop?" "Am I connected in some way to the other people?" "Am I even aware of them?" The two minutes pass, and the director says: "Let's run those four entrances in sequence now."

You run the blocking again, and from the private work you've been doing, you experiment with where you're coming from, where you're going and why. Someone misses an entrance, so you run it again. This gives you another chance to experiment.

After that, the director asks: "Any questions?" Before you can even chime in, one of your castmates asks: "Do we see each other?" The director replies: "I don't know. Let's try it both ways. First, let's say you do." "Okay, now let's say you are *not* aware of each other." "We'll go with the second choice for now." You just ran the move five times. You may not be back to this page in the script for a few days. Do you really want to have used this valuable rehearsal time to just walk from one spot to another?

The next scene doesn't involve you. So, you take your script and score, sit against the wall, and work. You make notes on what you just did and what you just found. You look ahead in your script to the next thing that involves you, to make sure you're ready for it. Then, you study the vocal parts you learned yesterday, or you analyze a lyric your character sings as we've done throughout this book, asking questions about it, looking for clues about your role.

* * *

My second show with Marvin was "Imaginary Friends," a "play with songs" by Nora Ephron, directed by Jack O'Brien. It opened on Broadway a year after "Sweet Smell of Success" and starred Cherry Jones as Mary McCarthy and Swoosie Kurtz as Lillian Hellman, in a story about their famous feud. The songs were written in various vaudeville styles, to comment on, or punctuate, the text. Act II opened with Lillian and Mary doing a number written in the style of a Shirley Temple song.

Prior to working on this show, I had thought Cherry Jones was the finest stage actress I had ever seen. I still think so. Getting to observe and be part of her process was a feast for an acting teacher. One day, out of town at the Old Globe in San Diego, the director asked the two stars if they'd like to end rehearsal early. Cherry jumped in with: "Please let's keep working. I haven't found my character yet."

On opening night in New York, she confided in me that the key she was looking for was found in one of my lyrics, a line she sang in our Shirley Temple song: "All that lonely loneliness is through." Mary was lonely as a child, and almost everything she did as an adult was done in response to this.

* * *

Write a history for your character, and be specific. What is said about the character in the play, by others and by yourself? Write about the people of importance in the character's life (family, friends, rivals, loves) and about your character's relationships with every other character in the play. Make a list of questions, based on details in the script.

For example, if you refer to a dog at one point, what kind of dog is it? How well do you (or did you) know the dog? What does this animal do when it sees you? Go to "Google Images," find a photo of a dog that feels right to you, so when you mention the dog, *that's* the one you're referring to. It may only be a passing reference in the play, but now "dog" is not just a one-syllable word; it's a creature your character has a history with.

* * *

If you are in the ensemble, know that you are not invisible; you are not a cog in a machine, a stage prop, or a *type* of person. Give your character or characters names. Why do they do what they do? The parts you sing and the moves you make may be designed to form a larger construct, but that doesn't mean the characters you play see themselves that way.

Looking out a ninth-floor window at the flow of people on a sidewalk below, you can see a certain ever-changing geometry in the patterns they make. But each one of those individuals knows what they're doing and where they're going. Are they late for an appointment, or looking for the right address, or dodging a bike messenger, or practicing for a job interview, or walking to meet the love of their life on the southwest corner?

You can bring this specificity of purpose to every moment of your chorus track. You will dance better and you will sing better. Your line in the vocal score may say "Cheerleader #3" or "Pirate #2," but you can play them as people.

Cheerleader #3 becomes Alyse, who had acne until she was 15 and moved to Spofford where she now attends Spofford High. She has destroyed all record of herself with bad skin, except for two online photos from 8th grade, which her younger brother Gil threatens to bring to light whenever he and his sister argue.

Alyse is secretly in love with Cheryl, a fellow cheerleader, but dates a senior boy, Frank. Frank is trying to decide whether to go to college in California next fall or go in-state and live at home. Every time Frank and Alyse talk about the subject, she encourages him to follow his dream and go to California. This causes him to talk about marriage, which enrages her. Alyse and Cheryl have occasional sleepovers, and they have one planned for this coming weekend.

Pirate #2 is named Paolo. He was found sleeping in an alley, half-starved at the age of 7. He was taken in and raised by a pirate named Willem, who then died of heart failure on the boy's 16th birthday. Paolo loves keeping watch in the crow's nest because he gets to be alone, feels like he's flying, and communes with the dead Willem. He used to be bullied by a pirate named Pick, but after practicing in private for 3 years, he outdueled Pick and then spared his life. He knows every constellation in the sky and uses snuff whenever he can get it.

If you do this kind of work on your ensemble roles, everything those characters do will be informed by it.

Note: You may be tempted to share this character work with your castmates, but this temptation should be resisted. Sharing these details might be fun, but it will turn them into backstage anecdotes, and they will cease to be useful.

For the same reason, making up parodies of the songs in the show can degrade your investment in them onstage. Parodies may be funny at the moment, but why paint graffiti on your own house?

* * *

When rehearsing a new show, changes come quickly and often. So, stay engaged, and understand that the more you bring to your work, the more the creative team will be able to see and assess their own. This will make the show better and make you a valued part of it.

Question: If you were the composer-lyricist, and you just wrote a new solo section for an ensemble number, to whom would you give it?

Answer: Someone you know will take good care of it.

* * *

If you are an understudy or standby, it is common for you to get zero rehearsal time in the role you're covering until the show opens. The catch is, you may be needed to go on in the role *before* then. So, what do you do?

You rehearse yourself. You watch, absorb, make notes about your character, what they're doing, what they want, what they know and don't know, and you practice, all the time. You get work-recordings made of the songs. The assistant musical director is a good person to go to for this. You attend as many rehearsals involving the character you're understudying as possible and keep up on all changes to blocking, text, music, choreography. And you find a way to run the show once a day, by yourself.

If you are a swing, covering say six or seven tracks, concentrate on one at a time. Make staging charts that show each character's movements, to develop an understanding of their spatial relationship to the whole picture. Know your vocal parts, your staging, and choreography. As a swing, your first job is to be in the right place. There can be a shot-out-of-a-cannon excitement each time you go on in a new track. I'll often hear a student say with pride: "I swung four tracks last weekend. In one performance, I was two different people." I honestly don't know how they do it. I would find the mathematics of the job truly impossible. In terms of acting, the process has allowed you little or no time for it, so keep it simple. Who are you? Why do you enter? What are you doing?

It's Halloween, 2005, a Monday night. Lisa and I are trick-or-treating in New Jersey with my daughter and a friend of hers. A cellphone rings.

Lisa is in previews for a new Broadway musical at the Marriott Marquis called "The Woman in White" (music by Andrew Lloyd Webber, lyrics by David Zippel, book by Charlotte Jones, direction by Trevor Nunn). The show has just played its first four previews, and the star (Maria Friedman, reprising her role from the London production) has gotten word that she needs surgery and will be out for at least a week, starting Thursday night. Lisa is her understudy.

Costumes will be overnighted from London, and Lisa will be given seven hours of rehearsal time before her first performance.

You know those chemical shifts I spoke of earlier when we first talked about "preparation?" Well, I saw Lisa have one of those upon hearing this news, on a New Jersey sidewalk, dressed as a witch.

Maria's surgery went perfectly, as did Thursday night's performance. The creative team and producers were thrilled and grateful. But that's not the point of the story. The point is, if you're an understudy, *be ready!*

Note: Later that night, Lisa said she told herself before her first entrance: "Take it one moment at a time."

* * *

During the run of a show, it is not uncommon to be given notes on your performance.

Take the notes, implement them, and allow your work to be more technical in those spots for a couple of days as you assimilate the notes. You will soon be able to get back to living your scenes and songs more seamlessly.

But in the meantime, remember how we talked about "re-upping" to your action when you've been distracted by something? This is another situation in which that technique can be invaluable.

* * *

When trying to repeat an especially good performance, the temptation is always to try to repeat the good results or to recapture how it felt. When you do this, you are aiming at a target, and even though you yourself have set the target, the performance will not be as good.

The thing to do is to repeat the process that led to the good performance, and that will give you your best chance of having *another* good performance.

* * *

Some of the most coveted jobs in your profession are as replacements in long-running shows. Whether playing a principal role or replacing in the ensemble, these jobs give you a year or more (sometimes, much more) of steady employment, during which time you can pay off debts, study, do workshops and breathe easier. And best of all, you are a "working actor."

The rehearsal process for replacements differs from show to show, but in most cases, you will be rehearsing with stage managers and resident directors. The direction you receive as a replacement will tend to be more prescriptive than on a new show. But as long as you work at the necessary pace and are respectful of needing to fit into an ongoing production, you will probably have some interpretive leeway.

In preparation for taking over a role, you will no doubt watch a good number of performances. It's normal to assume that the production team wants you to be like the actor who's currently playing the role. But this assumption can be needlessly limiting, and it may not even be true. The people in charge may actually be looking forward to the change, as an opportunity to sharpen or refocus their show, so listen to what is said in rehearsal and trust what you hear. And regardless of the speed of the process and the sometimes prescriptive nature of the direction, don't leave your acting skills and *yourself* out of the work.

* * *

I worked as an actor for a time when I was 19 and 20. My first professional job was playing The Boy in "The Fantasticks" off-Broadway, during the tenth year of the show's original forty-year run. A wise castmate named Charlie Goff noticed my onstage attention start to waver after a few months. He took me aside and offered this choice piece of advice: "They made the first move; they bought a ticket. We owe them a show." I should have figured that out for myself, but at 19, I hadn't.

I share this experience from 1969 at the Sullivan Street Playhouse to contrast the lack of tolerance I now have for actors short-changing the audience, the play, and themselves by not doing their best.

If you are in a long run and you find yourself less than fully invested onstage, you can start your process over, with tonight's performance. Look at your first entrance, your first scene, your first piece of singing and explore it again. Start there, and over the next week or two, work through the entire show.

You can do eight shows a week using muscle-memory and what I earlier called "the convenience of artifice." But it's no fun. The work is the fun.

Take the time you need to warm up your voice and your body, to center yourself and prepare. There's an *excited calm* in which we do our best work, and each of us is responsible for creating that for ourselves.

10

IN CONCERT

As a singing actor, you are often asked to perform in concerts. Some of you (by nature or experience) may be totally at home on the concert stage, but I often find that musical theater actors and students of the craft may find themselves less than certain of what they're doing in this medium.

As a point of comparison, there is one key element that concert work has in common with auditioning. You need to be truly present. You have to actually be there. If you leave yourself offstage and send some ghost out there to take your place, the performance will not be effective.

But if you are successful in achieving the level of "there-ness" needed in concert, it can then be taken back with you to your theater work and can improve every aspect of what you do as an actor.

Whether it's in a 50-seat club, a conventional theater of one size or another, or a concert hall, if you are outside the structure of a musical and you are singing a song in front of people, you are most likely doing one of four things: telling a story, playing a scene, entertaining, or being one of the musicians.

They all work, but it's best to know which one (or perhaps which combination of them) you're doing. And since concert work is not your main occupation, it's quite common for an actor not to know. "Telling a story" and "playing a scene" are obviously the closest to the subject of this book and are the stances you'll use most often, but the others can be useful as well.

* * *

Telling a Story

In concert, any song that *can* be sung as a story probably *should* be. The action is clear, and it puts you in direct communication with your audience. Like good theater, concert work is at its best when the elements at hand are used with economy, and in this situation, the elements are a story, an audience, and you.

Actors new to doing concerts often think they would feel more comfortable singing their story *above* the audience. Invariably, in class, this is how an actor will begin their exploration of such a song for an upcoming concert performance.

This is an understandable impulse, since you are used to doing this at auditions and in most musicals. But in a concert setting, choosing to sing a story above the audience is usually a choice made in fear, fear that looking directly at your audience might make you feel exposed and uncomfortable. At first, it *might* feel that way, but as with many situations in your work and your life, letting yourself be truly seen and known can lead to the most rewarding results.

Looking at some of the songs referenced in this book, Bill Finn's "And They're Off," James Taylor's "Millwork," and my song "What You'd Call A Dream" are obviously stories. They were written to be that. But what about Kander and Ebb's "A Quiet Thing," which, in its original context, Flora sings to herself and the universe? And how about Sondheim's "Finishing the Hat," where George is alone, singing to himself and the paint-scented air of his studio about the irreconcilable differences between his work and his relationship with Dot?

Sung in concert, "A Quiet Thing" is just begging to be shared with the audience and, as referenced earlier, "Finishing the Hat" can *also* be sung as a story; an impassioned one, but a story all the same. None of this is to suggest that in singing any of these songs to your audience you would stay riveted to them. This point came up before, when we were discussing how to play to invisible partners. We don't stay riveted to the people we're speaking to. Natural behavior takes us away, for any number of reasons, and like so many things in acting, this movement does not need to be planned – it just happens.

Playing a Scene

For concert purposes, I believe that a "scene" is any song that is clearly being sung to a specific other person. By this definition, Sara Bareilles' "Gravity" is a scene. It begins with the line: "Something always brings me back to you," and it so clearly feels like it's being sung to the *idea* of another person, in part because the lyric itself keeps coming back to the word "you."

If you watch a video of any of Sara Bareilles' live performances of this song, you will see that she is singing *above* the audience. Her partner in the song is in her head and her heart, so wherever her gaze happens to go, the other person goes with her. There is no external focal point as there might be if one were using this song for an audition.

Not to oversimplify this, but in concert work the presence of the word "you" frequently seems to be a determining factor in what makes a song a scene. "I Can't Make You Love Me," "Desperado," "My Heart Is So Full of You," "See I'm Smiling," and countless other songs feature the word "you" early and often, and this language does much to make them feel like scenes.

But how do you handle a song like "Anyone Can Whistle," which feels like a story until the last verse, when it seems to become a scene, with such lines as "Maybe you could show me . . ." and "Maybe if you whistle, whistle for me."

You could treat the whole song as a scene and sing it "away from us." Or you might treat the song as a story but subtly "leave us" for the last verse (or at least for those lines that are directed to the other person). Or you could sing the whole song directly to the audience.

But if you did that (sang the whole song to the audience), would that mean when you say "Maybe you could show me . . ." that you were literally asking the audience for help with this problem?

Not necessarily. Unlike the "acting" we've been talking about throughout this book, the concert stage is sometimes governed by a completely different set of principles, as in the stance that follows.

Entertaining (the Verb, Not the Adjective)

This is a widely used performance style in concert work, and it has nothing to do with whether the songs you're singing are stories or scenes. It is a technique that is, and has been, used by some of the most successful performers in the concert world. In this stance, a performer might sing everything directly to their audience, whatever the subject, whatever the perspective of the writing.

This is what Beyoncé is doing in her live performances. But it's also what Margaret Whiting did, what Lady Gaga usually does, what Sammy Davis, Jr. did, and what thousands of other concert artists have done since the idea of "putting on a show" was first imagined. And in each set of hands, it's done differently.

For example, the production values of Beyoncé's 2020 Live Concert are extraordinary, with gorgeous sets, up-to-the-moment lighting, terrific dancers (including the star) doing terrific choreography, and first-rate musical arrangements played by first-rate musicians. But even with all of this going on, the brightest thing on the stage is Beyoncé's presence, or rather how "present" she is. She obviously loves her audience, and they love her back, and the circular energy this creates seems to demand the direct contact of her performing style.

Margaret Whiting was a major recording star in the 1940s, 50s, and beyond, and a concert and cabaret star throughout the rest of the 20th century. She, too, was "entertaining," in that she sang every song directly to the audience, regardless of its content.

Singing from The Great American Songbook in a clean, clear voice (even in her later years), she was meticulous in her attention to the music and lyrics. Her father, Richard Whiting, was a noted composer of popular songs, and her mentor, Johnny Mercer, was one of the finest lyricists of all time. Perhaps because of this background, much of Whiting's performing style came from seeming to be the "messenger" between the songwriters whose work she sang and the audience.

Looking at Lady Gaga's 2020 Live Concert, she too is singing directly to her audience, but in this particular show, she starts out with a definite sense of separation between herself and her fans, a separation that becomes less and less as the concert goes on. Given her prowess as an entertainer, this is obviously a choice she and her director made, and it has the dynamic effect of giving the audience more and more of the person they came to see as the concert progresses.

There's a video of a Lady Gaga performance in Las Vegas (1/27/19) where she invites Bradley Cooper (her co-star in the film "A Star is Born") up onstage to sing the song "Shallow" with her.

I wrote in Chapter 4 that "the more you make the scene about the other person, the more we see *you*." That's what happens in this 8-minute guest spot, and it illuminates the singer more than anything else I've seen her do.

Sammy Davis, Jr. has been called "the greatest entertainer of all time." He sang and danced like no one else, and, most of the time, he addressed his audience directly. Occasionally, though, his work was so theatrical that he seemed to be using a traditional fourth wall. If you want to see him at his very best, there's a concert he did in Paris for UNICEF in 1985. It can be found online in a video series: "The Best of Sammy Davis, Jr. in the '80s." At approximately an hour and 45 minutes into the concert, he sings "Old Man River." In the song's introductory verse, he's telling a story to the audience. Then, as the body of the song begins, he seems to go inward while at the same time looking out where the river might be. He sings the rest of the song from this stance, and it is thrilling.

Being One of the Musicians

I don't recall how it began, but there was a five or six-year stretch in the 1990s when, once a year, my good friend Michael Kerker (of ASCAP) would take Henry Mancini, Dorothy Loudon, and me to see Rosemary Clooney at Rainbow & Stars, atop the RCA building in New York. Clooney (a truly great singer from Margaret Whiting's generation) performed from the stance of "being one of the musicians" late in her illustrious career, and watching her do this was a masterclass in the technique. If you watch a video of any of her work in the 1990s, you will see her wearing glasses. The glasses, and almost everything about her performances in this period, seemed to be saying: "I'm just part of the band. My instrument is my voice."

At first, when watching the video of Eminem's 2019 concert in Abu Dhabi, I would have said that he was "entertaining." The high energy of his performance, his direct address of the audience, and his constant movement around the stage suggested as much.

But the movement was unstructured (more like a random expelling of energy), and his patented gestures and body language similarly spoke of something unstructured and ambient.

What *was* specific and pointed in its purpose was Eminem's vocal delivery of his lyrics. It was deliberate and crisp. That was the first clue that he was "being one of the musicians" more than he was "entertaining." The second clue came from the lighting design. There was often as much light shining from upstage toward the audience as there was coming from out front, illuminating the star.

Watching the concert again, I caught a final clue, one I had missed the first time around. The clothes Eminem wore throughout the concert perfectly matched the tone of the material, but the choice to wear both a baseball cap and a hoodie in the first 15 minutes may have had an additional purpose.

Many of Eminem's peers wear baseball caps when they perform, but none of them that I could find wear both a baseball cap and a hoodie. And while we see this style all the time on the street, we don't tend to see it onstage (with the exception of Eminem), because the combination of the two types of headwear can obscure the performer's face from us.

So, like Rosemary Clooney's glasses, he might be telling us something. He might be saying: "I appear to be putting on a show, but I think of myself as one of the musicians, and my instrument is my writing."

I saw John Pizzarelli (the brilliant jazz guitarist and singer) and Daniel Jobim (grandson of the great Brazilian composer Antonio Carlos Jobim) in concert at the Blue Note in New York in 2018. They were doing a 50th anniversary celebration of an album Daniel's grandfather had recorded with Frank Sinatra.

The two of them sat on low stools at the edge of the stage, Pizzarelli cradling his guitar, and Jobim wearing a funky fedora. Mostly, they focused their gaze on their vocal mics, or even the floor, not out of any kind of shyness, but to define what they were doing. The performance wasn't about their eyes; it was about voices (the composer's voice, the two singers, and the guitar). But it was also about ears. You could see the two musicians actively listening to one another and, by example, inviting us to engage in exactly the same way.

***

Janis Ian singing "At Seventeen" (in 1976 at "Old Grey Whistle Test") is "telling a story." This performance is as good as musical storytelling gets.

Sarah Vaughn singing "Lush Life" at the North Sea Jazz Festival (12/7/81) is "being one of the musicians" while also somehow living the story.

Harry Connick, Jr. "In Concert on Broadway" (2010) is "entertaining" when he's out in front of the band, singing. But when he's playing the piano and singing, he "becomes one of the musicians," and not just because he's playing an instrument. When he's at the piano, the actual purpose of his singing changes. It becomes less about personality and more about the music itself, and for him, this seems to be his natural habitat.

John Legend singing "Ordinary People" (in 2013, "Live on Letterman") is playing piano, focusing his gaze about a foot above the vocal mic, and clearly thinking of the person he is singing to. He is "playing a scene."

After each chorus ("We're just ordinary people"), there is a section that says: "Take it slow, take it slow. . . ." For these sections, he encourages the audience to sing, and they do. In doing this, he moves effortlessly from "playing a scene" to "entertaining," then repeats the sequence, then finishes the song to the unseen partner. This all happens so smoothly that one could miss all the movement between the different stances, but it is there, and it's beautiful.

Ciara singing "Thinkin Bout You" at the 2019 Billboard Awards is "playing a scene" in a very stylized way while "entertaining."

Pink singing "Glitter in the Air" at the 2010 Grammy Awards begins with a very contained form of "entertaining," which then segues into a kind of performance-art (complete with aerial work and a waterfall), and it works.

Linda Ronstadt singing "Desperado" (in 1977 in Atlanta) is "playing a scene" while alternately directing her gaze at the microphone and closing her eyes. Unlike what Pizzarelli and Jobim were saying by looking at their mics, Ronstadt is saying: "This is a very private scene."

Stevie Wonder is "being the music" and radiating the joy this gives him. There is so much great video of him performing live. My favorites are "World Rock Live" (2015) and "Live at Musikladen" (1974).

Frank Sinatra, early in his career (1940s), was a handsome, young band singer with all the postures and attitudes appropriate to this role. But somewhere in the early 1950s, he started "telling stories" and "playing scenes," which is then what he did for the rest of his long career. His persona and his swagger may suggest that he was "entertaining," and at times he was. But mostly he was playing scenes and telling stories. See Madison Square Garden (1974) "My Way" for great storytelling.

So much of the discussion above is about knowing what it is you're doing on the concert stage and about letting the audience know too so they can receive it. You can then, of course, surprise them, as John Legend and Pink did in the performances referenced above. But "making sense," doing what feels right for you, for the material, and for the venue, brings a clarity to the endeavor that can make any concert appearance successful.

* * *

You've been asked to sing a song in a concert featuring the work of 3 or 4 young theater composers. Coaching the song with someone you trust is always useful in this situation, as there may tend to be very little formal rehearsal. As you work on the material, picture the space you'll be performing in. This is especially valuable if the song is a story.

Will the audience be right in front of you, or are they perhaps on three sides? How high is the stage? Is there a balcony?

Will you be using the microphone in a stand or are you thinking of holding it in your hand? Generally, if you are less experienced with concert work, having the mic in the stand might be preferable because this allows you a physicality that is closer to what you are accustomed to in your theater work. If you *are* going to hold the mic, try rehearsing with a prop of some kind, so you get used to having the object in your hand.

As you rehearse with your "mic," treat it as though it is only there to amplify your voice. Let it almost disappear. We've all seen seasoned rock performers and nightclub singers engage in one sort of stylized mic-behavior or another. For the singing actor who is "telling a story" or "playing a scene," this type of business will only detract from your performance.

Now, let's say the song you've been asked to sing in this concert is a duet. Chances are that, being a duet, it is some kind of a "scene." There may be a director, or the staging may be left entirely to you and your scene partner. Rehearse together, just as you would for an acting class, and decide how you, as a team, want to approach the song.

Will you be looking at each other, or will you be facing out, or perhaps some combination of the two? Consider the sightlines in the room and how you want to use the mics.

The day of the concert, you will most likely have a rehearsal of some sort in the space. Actually being in the room, you may change your idea of how the song should be staged, or you may be *asked* to do it differently.

Stay loose and open in this rehearsal. The process will no doubt be quick, but as long as the choices being made make sense to you, you'll be able to do good work.

The day *before* the concert, one of the performers drops out, and you are asked to learn and sing an additional song. This happens all the time.

Take a breath, and just do it. You have resources that haven't been tapped yet. Tap them here, and you'll be able to bring them back to your theater work with you. Think how useful an extra measure of flexibility and confidence would be to you in your next audition, or in the play rehearsals you're about to begin, or the 8-show week that starts Tuesday night.

I chose this hypothetical concert featuring the work of 3 or 4 young theater composers for two reasons. First, because it's a type of concert that you (the singing actor) are frequently asked to participate in. I could just as easily have focused the discussion on any of the common concert opportunities that come up for actors, such as benefits, or concerts honoring a noted composer, or concept-evenings, like Scott Siegel's "Broadway by the Year" series at New York's Town Hall.

Instead, I chose the young composers event to highlight another value of singing in such a concert. It's very possible that none of these young writers saw you in your recent, off-Broadway show. Well, now they've *all* seen you, and each one of these writers or teams has at least two musicals they're in the process of writing. And they will be doing workshops, demos, and first productions of these shows in the very near future. If you do well in the concert, I promise you they will think of you when casting.

* * *

A different concert: you are asked to sing back-up with two other people in an evening of rock songs written by a talented friend. Say yes, feel the music in your body as you sing and enjoy "being one of the musicians."

* * *

A different, different concert: you are an actor who has started writing songs and are going to be performing two of them in concert. This is not only an opportunity to have your songs heard; it's an opportunity to let your performing be more about the material than it is about *you*. This shift of focus off of yourself can be liberating and so instructive to you as an actor.

I've been guiding you in this book to "sing the words." This remains true even when you are the author. You know where these songs came from, what the original reason to sing was, even if you never articulated that to yourself. It is stored inside you and in the very substance of the songs. This information is now yours to use in your performance.

* * *

You've been invited to be a guest singer in a "Pops" concert with a symphony orchestra. You will be doing a 3-song set for which your agent/manager has negotiated a lucrative fee. You may be asked to sing specific songs, or you may be given a list of some 10–20 titles to choose from. These are songs the orchestra has existing arrangements of, that suit the subject and tone of this particular concert.

With the conductor's help, you devise a set. In choosing, look for variety and sing-ability (the keys may or may not be negotiable). If I were doing the choosing, I would pick a song that is a scene, a song that is a story, and a song where the orchestra gets to let loose.

Your 3-song set may be the only time in the evening when the audience gets to hear a singing voice and songs with words. Because of this, you will be singing for ears that are fresh and people who are happy to see you.

Once again, it's best to get help from a coach or a trusted friend as you prepare for this outing. Your rehearsal time in the space will be limited, as will your time with the orchestra, so try to know what you're doing before you get there.

If I were coaching or directing you, here's what I would offer. When your song is a story, really tell the audience a story. Before you begin, take in the room and the audience. "How should I say this?" "What do I want to tell these people?" Early in the song, sing a couple of lines to the first few rows. If you start by singing to the back of the house, the audience may not know you're actually singing to them, because singing to the back of the house looks virtually the same as singing *above* the audience. Once they know you're telling this story to *them*, you can play to any part of the house. The direct communication you've now established will bring the audience toward you. You can feel it happen.

When you're playing a scene, really play a scene. You can use a tight visual focus above the audience if it suits the material, or you can do what Sara Bareilles does with "Gravity." In this approach, you are also singing above the audience, but your partner in the scene is inside you, so wherever your gaze goes, the partner goes with you.

By clearly differentiating between stories and scenes, you cause the concert hall to figuratively shift back and forth between feeling like a living room and feeling like a theater. All of the above (from singing to the front rows early in a story, to the different ways of playing a scene) hold true in *any* size room, from a 50-seat cabaret to a 3,000-seat concert hall.

Now, for the song in your "Pops" set where the orchestra gets to let loose. Given the tone of the arrangement, you may feel that you are supposed to be an "entertainer" in this song, that the skills you bring as an actor are not sufficient for the occasion.

But even in this song, you can be telling a story or playing a scene. However, the act of being "truly present" now takes on an additional aspect. The reality of this moment is that having all that rhythm and sound behind you feels great. Let it feel great, and let yourself feel the music in your body as you sing. The audience is feeling it; you can too. As long as you do that, you can be "telling a story," "playing a scene," or (if it feels right to you) "entertaining."

The orchestra will probably have an instrumental break in this number. When this occurs, do what the reality of the moment is telling you to do. Turn and face them, and enjoy the music. In a sense, you become an onstage member of the audience when you do this, adding yet another stance to your set.

More than likely, you will also be speaking to the audience. As a guest singer in a "Pops" concert, the need for this is minimal. But, as with everything you do in this medium, really do it. You can talk about anything: the orchestra, the hall, your hotel, the Broadway show you're in, the next song, your *shoes*! But really do it.

* * *

It's 2011. Maddy Jarmon is singing Leonard Cohen's "Hallelujah" in class for the first time. She is a new student, 18 years old, newly transplanted from Texas to New York, and she possesses one of the most beautiful contemporary voices I have ever heard. "Hallelujah" has four verses and choruses, of which Maddy sings the first three. The song is very much a scene, between the singer and whomever they are singing to, but we discover that, for Maddy, the partner is different in each of the three verses; it's *three* scenes.

Looking at my notes from her years in class, I see that between 2011 and 2015 Maddy revisited this song about once a year, much to the delight of her Tuesday evening classmates. And throughout those years, her invisible partners for the first and second verses remained firm, while her third verse partner would change over time.

It's 2019, and I haven't seen Maddy since she was last in class, in 2015. I'm talking on the phone with my dear friend, Deric Rosenblatt (one of New York's premier vocal coaches, and Maddy's vocal coach since 2012).

He asks me if I've been watching her on NBC's "The Voice." She is now using the name Maelyn Jarmon, is about half-way through the competition, and has, apparently, been doing extremely well on the show.

I tune in and, this week, she is singing "Hallelujah." The show has lavish production values and a live audience that is noisy and appreciative. Maelyn is perched on a large staircase that is lit from within, singing better than ever, and inhabiting the three verses as three different scenes. No one watching this deeply focused performance would ever have known that's what she was doing, and that's as it should be.

Also as it should be, a few weeks later, the winner of Season 16 of "The Voice" is announced, and it's Maelyn.

* * *

Sutton Foster and Megan McGinnis stand next to each other on the stage of Carnegie Hall (3/13/15) looking straight out above the audience, singing "Flight." They are each having a private experience, separate from the other, yet interwoven musically.

The song was written as a solo, but back in 2008, Michael Rafter (Sutton's musical director) put together a gorgeous duet arrangement for the two women. It appears on Sutton's debut album, "Wish," and she and Megan continue to sing it in concerts around the country.

Ironically, someone asked me recently: "Can that song be sung as a solo?"

11

IN CONCLUSION

"Flight"
Music & Lyrics by Craig Carnelia (1992)

Let me run through a field in the night
Let me lift from the ground
Till my soul is in flight
Let me sway like the shade of a tree
Let me swirl like a cloud
In a storm on the sea
Wish me on my way
Through the dawning day
I wanna flow, wanna rise, wanna spill
Wanna grow in a grove
On the side of a hill

I don't care if the train runs late
If the checks don't clear
If the house blows down

I'll be off where the weeds run wild
Where the seeds fall
Far from this earthbound town
And I'll start to soar
Watch me rain till I pour
I'll catch a ship
That'll sail me astray
Get caught in a wind
I'll just have to obey
Till I'm flying away

Ah - - - - - -
Ah - - - - - -

Let me leave behind
All the clouds in my mind
I wanna wake without wondering why
Finding myself in a burst for the sky
High - - - - - -

I'll just roll
Let me lose all control
I wanna float like a wish in a well
Free as the sound of the sea in a shell

I don't know but maybe I'm just a fool
I should keep to the ground
I should stay where I'm at
Maybe everyone has hunger like this
And the hunger will pass
But I can't think like that
All I know is
Somewhere through a clearing
There's a flickering of sunlight
On a river, long and wide
And I have such a river inside

Let me run through a field in the night
Let me lift from the ground
Till my soul is in flight

IN CONCLUSION

Let me sway like the shade of a tree
Let me swirl like a cloud
In a storm on the sea
Wish me on my way
Through the dawning day
I wanna flow, wanna rise, wanna spill
Wanna grow on the side of a hill
Wanna shift like a wave rollin' on
Wanna drift from the path
I've been trav'ling upon
Before I am gone

The music of this song gives the singer a chance to experience the very thing they say they want, while the lyric is, in some way, asking for permission. But from whom or what is this permission being asked? The person singing knows what they want but doesn't seem to know that the key to the prison is in their back pocket. So even though the song was not written for a character in a musical, we're once again dealing with what the character knows and what they don't know, and how the abrasion between the two propels the song.

In class, I had the opportunity to work on "Flight" with countless students, and though it only just now occurs to me, not one of them ever considered singing the song as anyone but themselves. The subject never even came up. The lyric is so oddly poetic that the song seems to become autobiographical for each person who sings it. In a way, this sort of "ownership" of your songs is what I've been guiding you to.

Throughout the book, we've talked about using yourself and your own experience to help you relate to everything from "Green Finch and Linnet Bird" and "My Stupid Mouth" to "Moon River," and how, at a certain point in their respective processes, the writer and the actor find themselves engaged in identical tasks. "Flight" seems to invite abundant use of these ideas, without my ever having intended it.

We are animals. We have instincts and impulses. And yet, we countermand this priceless information with second-guessing, inhibition, people-pleasing, and social conditioning of all kinds.

We guess what other people want us to be, so we can try to be it. And we think that if we can just control the product, the performance, we will be successful, happy, safe.

What would happen if you were not in charge of every moment? How scary would that be? Would it help you to know that you were *never* actually in charge? Because it's true.

Let yourself be caught off-guard. Let yourself be excited, intrigued, angry, confused, ecstatic, heartbroken. Let yourself be powerful.

Think of all the things you've done to keep your true self hidden and all the things you've pretended to be to make other people like you. Did any of it ever work?

I finished "Flight" in January, 1992. The next month, I began teaching.

CREDITS

"Millwork"
Written by James V. Taylor
© Country Road Music, Inc. (ASCAP)
ALL RIGHTS RESERVED. USED BY PERMISSION.

"My Heart Is So Full of You"
From "THE MOST HAPPY FELLA"
By Frank Loesser
© 1956 (Renewed) FRANK MUSIC CORP
This arrangement © 2020 FRANK MUSIC CORP
All Rights Reserved
Reprinted by permission of Hal Leonard LLC.

"Welcome to the Night"
From "SWEET SMELL OF SUCCESS"
Music by Marvin Hamlisch
Lyrics by Craig Carnelia
Lyrics Published by Big A Music LLC
(Administered by A. Schroeder International LLC)
Used by Permission, International Copyright Secured.

CREDITS

"At the Fountain"
From "SWEET SMELL OF SUCCESS"
Music by Marvin Hamlisch
Lyrics by Craig Carnelia
Lyrics Published by Big A Music LLC
(Administered by A. Schroeder International LLC)
Used by Permission, International Copyright Secured.

"Flight"
Music & Lyrics by Craig Carnelia
Published by Big A Music LLC
(Administered by A. Schroeder International LLC)
Used by Permission, International Copyright Secured.

INDEX

"A Day in Falsettoland" 13
"A Marriage Proposal" 13
A Star Is Born (2020) (film) 141
ABBA 81
Abbott, George 32–33
acapella 66–68
action 34–52; definition xv, 34; and music 43–44; practical 35–36
Adams, Lee 88, 101
"Adelaide's Lament" 101
Afton, Emily 118
Ahrens, Lynn 73
Ain't Too Proud (show) 82
Aladdin (show) 94
Albert, Fred 98
Al Hirschfeld Theatre 113
"All I Need Is One Good Break" 33
"All The Things You Are" 37, 92
An American in Paris (show) 13
Andersson, Benny 74
"And They're Off" 27–29, 138
"Angel From Montgomery" 118

Annie Get Your Gun 86
Anyone Can Whistle (show) 8
"Anyone Can Whistle" (song) 8–9, 120, 139
"Anytime" 13
"Arabian Nights" (song) 94
Arlen, Harold 68, 89, 90
artists, definition of 43
Ashford, Annaleigh 99–100
Ashman, Howard 80, 94
Assassins 78
"At Seventeen" 143
"At The Fountain" 124–128
auditioning 107–115; 16-bar cuts 113–114; direction 111; dress 111–112; feedback 114–115; hair 112; nuts and bolts of 108–111
Avenue Q 79

Bad Years, The 117
Baker's Wife, The 74
Bare 101
Bareilles, Sara 16, 70, 139, 148

INDEX

Beautiful (show) 83
Berlin, Irving 22, 84, 89, 90, 91
Bernstein, Leonard 43, 87, 101
Beyoncé 140
Big River 11
Blackwell, Otis 105
"Blame It on My Youth" 90
Blankson-Wood, Ato 16
"Bluebird" 70
Bock, Jerry 34, 35, 87
Bonds, D.B 95, 100
Bono, Stacie 121–122
Book of Mormon, The 79
Boublil, Alain 73
Bowles, Jennifer 118–119
Brackett, Stephen 117
Brescia, Lisa 43, 133
Brickman, Marshall 81
Brigadoon 85
Bright Star 11
Broadway By the Year 146
Brown, Jason Robert 48, 113
Bruni, Marc 83

Cabaret (show) 33, 88
Camelot (show) 86
Carlson-Goodman, Briana 113
Carmichael, Hoagy 89
Carnelia, Daisy 52, 117
Carnelia, James 116, 120
Carousel (show) 45, 68, 88
Caskey, Marilyn 96–97
"Changing My Major" 39–40, 114
Charles, Ray 93
Cherkaoui, Sidi Larbi 84
Cher Show, The 82
Chess 74
Chicago (show) 33
Ciara 144
Clooney, Rosemary 142, 143
"Cockeyed Optimist" 86

Cody, Diablo 84
Cohen, Leonard 149
Cohn, Ben 95
Coleman, Cy 71, 73
Collins, Kevin T. 16
Color Purple, The (show) 78
Comden, Betty 101
comedy 79; uptunes 90–91; funny songs 94–101
Company 77, 88, 96
"Compromise" 95, 97, 117
concerts 137–150; being one of the musicians 142–146; entertaining 140–144, 148; playing a scene 139–140, 143–144, 148; telling a story 138–139, 143, 147–148
Connick Jr., Harry 143
Contemporary Musical Theater 74–75, 77–79, 87–88, 92–93, 101; comedy 79; Disney 80; jukebox 80–84; pop-melodrama 79–80
"Contest, The" (song) 121
Cooley, Eddie 105
Cooper, Bradley 141
"Cornet Man" 113, 122
Covert, Kevin 98
Creighton, Robert 17
Crewe, Bob 81
Crowley, Bob 127
"Cry For Me" 83

Davis Jr, Sammy 140, 141
Dear Evan Hansen 33, 43
definitions xv, xvii
"Defying Gravity" 45, 73, 94
DeLugg, Milton 64, 90
"Desperado" 9–11, 139, 144
Diamonds 16
Dietz, Howard 89, 90
Dirty Rotten Scoundrels (show) 95
disbelief, suspension of 118

Disney 80
Disney musicals 14, 80
Dixon, Mort 90
Dreyfuss, Laura 33
dynamics 63–64

Ebb, Fred 32–33, 88, 101
Elice, Rick 81
Eliscu, Edward 74, 90
Ellington, Duke 89, 90
Eminem 142
ensemble roles 131–132
Ephron, Nora 130

Falsettos 13, 113
"Fanny Pack" 95, 99
Fantasticks, The 135
"Far From the Home I Love" 34–35, 37
Feldman, Jack 14
"Fever" 105
Fiddler On The Roof 34–35, 87
Fields, Dorothy 15, 73, 89, 90
"Finishing The Hat" (song) 45–46, 50–51, 138–139
Finke, Alex 15, 121
Finn, William 13, 27, 138
Fish, Daniel 85
Flaherty, Stephen 73
"Flight" 151–154
Flora The Red Menace 32–33
Floyd Collins 36–37
focal point: at auditions 112–113; in concert 137–150; use of invisible partners 102–106
Follies 12
Foster, Sutton 44, 45, 97, 149–150
Four Seasons, The 81, 82
Franklin, Aretha 74
Frey, Glenn 9, 10
Friedman, Maria 133
Fun Home 39–40

Funny Girl (show) 113
funny songs 94–101

"Gainesville" 74
Gaudio, Bob 81, 83
George, Don 90
Gershwin, George 84, 89, 90, 92
Gershwin, Ira 84, 89, 90, 92
Giant (show) 78
Gibson, William 88
"Gimme Gimme" 45, 51–52
"Glitter in The Air" 71, 144
Goff, Charlie 135
Goffin, Gerry 83
Goffman, Devon 17
Golden Age of Musical Theater 84–88
Golden Boy (show) 88, 101
Goldman, James 12
Goldrich, Zina 95, 117
"Goody, Goody" 90
"Gravity" (song) 16, 139, 148
Green, Adolf 101
"Green Finch and Linnet Bird" 15, 153
Greif, Michael 12
Guare, John 86
Guettel, Adam 36, 37, 71
Guys and Dolls 73, 85, 86, 101
Gypsy 87, 97, 114

Hadestown 78
Hair 77, 79, 85, 88, 113
"Hallelujah" (song) 149
Hamilton 41, 46, 79
Hamlisch, Marvin 86, 124, 125, 130, 156
Hammerstein, Oscar 25–26, 37–38, 68, 84, 92, 105
Hanley, James F. 90
Harburg, E. Y. 68
Harnick, Sheldon 34–35, 37, 76, 87
Hart, Lorenz 84, 89, 90, 101

Heathers (show) 101
Heisler, Marcy 95, 96, 117
Hellman, Lillian 130
"Hello Young Lovers" 47
Henley, Don 9, 10
Henningsen, Erika 101
Henry, Joshua 88
Heyman, Edward 90
Hicks, Michael 77
Hilliard, Bob 97
"History of Wrong Guys, The" 100
Hodges, Johnny 90
Holzman, Winnie 21
Horowitz, Leah 12
"How Glory Goes" 36–37
Hunt, Liana 14
Hytner, Nicholas 127

Ian, Janis 143
"I Can't Make You Love Me" 40–41
Iconis, Joe 101
"I Could Have Danced All Night" 5–8
"If I Loved You" 88
"If I Were King of The Forest" 122
"I Get a Kick Out of You" 92
"I Love a Piano" 90
"I Love to Cry at Weddings" 73
Imaginary Friends 130
"I'm Beginning To See The Light" 90
"I'm In Love With A Wonderful Guy" 86
In the Heights 41, 78
Into the Woods 71
"Is It Really Me?" 24–25, 25, 105
Is There Life After High School? 116
"It's Hard To Speak My Heart" 113
"Itsy Bitsy Teenie Weenie Yellow Polka Dot Bikini" 71
"I've Got the World On a String" 90
"I Want to Be Loved By You" 99
"I Want To Be With You" 101

"I Wish I Didn't Love You So" 90
"I Wish I Were in Love Again" 90

Jagged Little Pill (show) 84
James, Brian d'Arcy 124, 127–128
James, Harry 90
Jarmon, Maddy (Maelyn) 149
Jekyll and Hyde (show) 79
Jersey Boys (show) 81, 82, 83
Jobim, Antonio Carlos 143
Jobim, Daniel 143
"Joe" 119
Joel, Billy 74
Johnson, Catherine 81
Jones, Charlotte 133
Jones, Cherry 130
Jones, Rachel Bay 43
Jones, Tom 24, 26, 105
jukebox musicals 80–84

Kalmar, Bert 99
Kander, John 32–33, 88, 101, 138
Katz, Natasha 127
Kerker, Michael 142
Kern, Jerome 15, 89, 90, 92
Kerrigan, Kait 101, 117
Kindley, Jeffrey 116
King And I, The 25–26, 46–47, 121
King, Carole 83
Kinky Boots 100
Kitt, Tom 12
Klein, Alisa 97–98
Koehler, Ted 90
Krieger, Henry 68
Kron, Lisa 39–40
Kurtz, Swoosie 130

Lady Gaga 140, 141
Lahr, Bert 122
Lamont, Robin 61
Last Five Years, The 48–49
Laurents, Arthur 87

INDEX

Lee, Gypsy Rose 87
Legend, John 143–144
Lehrer, Tom 98
Leiber & Stoller 118
Leigh, Carolyn 71
Lennon, John 64
Lerner, Alan Jay 5
Les Misérables (show) 73, 79
"Let's Misbehave" 90
Levant, Oscar 90
Lewis, Sam 98
"Light in the Piazza, The" (song) 71
Lindsay, Kara 14
Lippa, Andrew 2
Lithgow, John 124
Little Mermaid, The (film) 80
Little Me (show) 71
Loesser, Frank 56, 62, 73, 90, 101, 155
Loewe, Frederick 5
Loudon, Dorothy 142
"Love Who You Love" 73
Lowdermilk, Brian 101, 117
Lucas, Craig 74
"Lush Life" 143

McAnuff, Des 81
McCarthy, Mary 130
McCartney, Paul 64
McDaniel, Sean 95
MacDermott, Galt 77
McGinnis, Megan 149–150
McGrath, Douglas 83
Malneck, Matty 90
"Mama Who Bore Me" 71
Mamma Mia! (show) 14, 81, 82
Mancini, Henry 52, 142
Mann, Barry 83
Mann, Billy 71
Man of No Importance, A 73
"Mark's All-Male Thanksgiving" 13
Masteroff, Joe 88
"Master of the House" 73

Matilda 119
Matlock, Victoria 105
Mayer, John 26, 101
"Meadowlark" 74, 75, 92
Mean Girls (show) 78, 101
Melrose, Ron 127
Menken, Alan 14, 80, 94
"Mention My Name in Sheboygan" 97
Mercer, Johnny 41, 52, 89, 90, 141
Merrill, Bob 113
Miller, Chris 101
"Million Dollar Baby" 90
Million Dollar Quartet 105
"Millwork" 54–56, 60–61, 128, 155
Miranda, Lin-Manuel 41, 101
Miss Saigon 79
Mitchell, Joni 101
Moby Dick (film) 116
Monroe, Marilyn 99–100
"Moon River" 52
Morgan, Betsy 46–47, 121–122
Morissette, Alanis 84
Most Happy Fella, The (show) 56, 155
Motown (show) 82
Mueller, Jessie 83, 88
music 53–75; acapella 66–68; acting the 53; learning 58–59, 128; pitch 64–65; rhythm 59–62; volume & dynamics 63–64
Music Man, The 85–86
My Fair Lady 5–8
"My Funny Valentine" 90
"My Heart Is So Full Of You" 56–57, 62–63, 72, 128, 155
"My Lord and Master" 26
Mysels, Sammy 97
"My Stupid Mouth" 26–27, 153
"My Way" 144

New Brain, A 27
Newman, Randy 74

INDEX

Newsies 14
"New York State of Mind" 74
Next To Normal 12
Nicholaw, Casey 96
"No Place Like London" 121
Northen, Lindsay 95, 117
No Strings (show) 87
Nunn, Trevor 85, 133

O'Brien, Cara 39
O'Brien, Jack 88, 130
Odets, Clifford 88
O'Hara, Kelli 46–47, 86, 121, 124
"Ohio" 101
Oklahoma (show) 84–85
"Oklahoma" (song) 97, 99
"Old Maid" 26
"Old Man River" 141
"One More Kiss" 12
110 in the Shade 24, 26, 105
"On the Other Side of the Tracks" 71
"On the Steps of the Palace" 71
On Your Feet! (show) 82
"Orange Colored Sky" 64, 90
Ordinary Days 78
"Ordinary People" (song) 143
"Over the Rainbow" 68

Pajama Game, The 86
Parade 113
Patinkin, Mandy 45
Paulus, Diane 84
"Pearl's A Singer" 118
Phantom of the Opera, The (show) 79
"Picture in the Hall, The" 74
Pink 71, 144, 145
Pins and Needles 96
"Pity the Child" 74
Pizzarelli, John 143, 144
play, ability to 116–122
Pockriss, Lee 71
"Poisoning Pigeons in the Park" 98

Porter, Cole 84, 89, 90, 92
Posey, Parker 99, 100
Poster Boy 114
practical action 35–36
preparation 19–33; asking yourself questions 23; definitions xv; and detail 24–26; failed 19–20; successful 20; purpose of 19, 33; scenario choice 22–23
Presley, Elvis 42, 105
Price, Paige 96
Prince, Harold (Hal) 16, 32, 77, 88
Prince, Josh 83
Prine, John 118
production 123–136; changes 132; the ensemble 131–132; performance notes 134; rehearsals 127–130, 132–133, 134–135; replacements 134–135; rough read/sing-through 129

"Quiet Thing, A" 32–33, 138–139

Rado, James 77
Rafter, Michael 150
Ragni, Gerome 77
"Rain in Spain, The" 7
Randy Newman's Faust 74
Reid, Mike 40
Rent 78
replacements 134–135
rhythm 59–63, 91, 92
Rice, Tim 74
Robber Bridegroom, The 11
Robbins, Jerome 87
rock and pop 92–94
Rodgers, Richard 25, 37, 68, 84, 87, 89, 90, 101, 105
Rome, Harold 96
Ronstadt, Linda 9, 144
Rose, Billy 74, 90
Rosenblatt, Deric 149
Rosenstein, Jaime 17

INDEX 163

Ruby, Harry 99
Russell, Bill 68
Russell, Robert 32

"Sadder but Wiser Girl, The" 85
Samonsky, Andrew 38
Sanford, Dick 97
Sater, Steven 71
Saturday Night Fever (show) 96
Scanlan, Dick 51
Schaeffer, Eric 12
Schmidt, Harvey 24, 105
Schönberg, Claude-Michel 73
Schwartz, Arthur 89, 90
Schwartz, Stephen 21, 74
"See I'm Smiling" 48–49
sexy songs xvi
"Shallow" 141
Shamblin, Allen 40
Shankman, Hannah 94
Sheik, Duncan 71
She Loves Me (show) 76
"She Loves Me" (song) 76
Sher, Bartlett 86
"Shine On Your Shoes, A" 90
Show Boat (show) 46
Side Show 68, 95
Siegel, Scott 146
sight-reading 58
Sinatra, Frank 143, 144
"Sit Down, You're Rockin' the Boat" 73
16-bar auditions 113–114
Smokey Joe's Café 118
"Soliloquy" 45, 68
Some Like It Hot (film) 100
"Some People" 114
"Something's Coming" 43–46, 62, 72
Sondheim, Stephen 8, 10, 12, 15, 45, 50, 71, 77, 87, 96, 114, 138
South Pacific 37–38, 86, 105
Spamalot 98
Spitfire Grill, The 11

Spring Awakening 71
standards 59, 84, 88–92
Stanley, Elizabeth 105
Stein, Willie 64, 90
Stevens, Marcus 97
Stothart, Herbert 99
Strouse, Charles 88, 101
Styne, Jule 87, 113, 114
Summer (show) 82
Sunday In The Park With George 45, 50
Sweeney Todd 15, 80, 121–122
Sweet Charity 73
Sweet Smell Of Success (show) 86, 124–128, 130, 155–156

Tapestry (album) 83
Taylor, James 54–55, 60–61, 138, 155
Taylor, Samuel 87
Temple, Shirley 130
Temptations, The 82
Terkel, Studs 119
Tesori, Jeanine 39–40, 51
"They All Laughed" 90
"They Can't Take That Away From Me" 92
"Think" 74, 92
"Thinkin Bout' You" 144
"This is My 16 Bars" 97–98, 99
Thoroughly Modern Millie (show) 45, 51
Three Postcards 74
Tina (show) 82
Tracz, Joe 114
Traditional Musical Theater 75, 82, 84–88, 100–101
Trujillo, Sergio 81
Tveit, Aaron 11–12
Tysen, Nathan 101

Ulvaeus, Bjorn 74
understudies 132–134
up-tempo songs 90–91

INDEX

Uranowitz, Brandon 13, 113
Urinetown 79

Vance, Paul 71
Vaughn, Sarah 143
Violet 11
Voice, The (NBC series) 149
volume 63–64
von Mayrhauser, Peter 127

Waiting For Guffman 99–100
Waitress (show) 16, 78
Warren, Harry 89, 90
"Watch What Happens" 14
"Way You Look Tonight, The" 16, 90
Webber, Andrew Lloyd 133
Weed, Barrett Wilbert 101
Weil, Cynthia 83
"We Kiss In A Shadow" 25–26
"Welcome To The Night" 124, 155–156
West Side Story (show) 43–44, 46, 87
"What Is It About Her?" 2–5
"What'll I Do?" 22–24, 51, 91–92
"What More Can I Say?" 13
"What You'd Call a Dream" 17, 138
Wheeldon, Christopher 13
"When I Fall In Love" 90
"When I Grow Up (The G-man Song)" 96
"When I'm 64" 64
"When the Sun Comes Out" 90
White, Ted 74

Whiting, Margaret 140, 142
Whiting, Richard 141
"Who Played Poker With Pocahontas When John Smith Went Away" 98
Wicked 17, 21, 45
Wild Party, The 2–6
"Without A Song" 74, 90
Wizard And I, The 21, 22
Wizard Of Oz, The (film) 68, 122
Woman In White, The (show) 133–134
Wonderful Town 101
Wonder, Stevie 144
Working (show) 54, 60–61, 119

Yorkey, Brian 12
"You Are Love" 37
"You Could Drive a Person Crazy" 96
"You Gotta' Get A Gimmick" 97
"You Should Be Loved" 68
"You've Got That Thing" 90
Youmans, Vincent 74, 90
Young, Joe 98
Young, Victor 90
"Younger Than Springtime" 37–38, 105

Zachary, Noah 17
"Zing, Went the Strings of My Heart" 90
Zippel, David 133